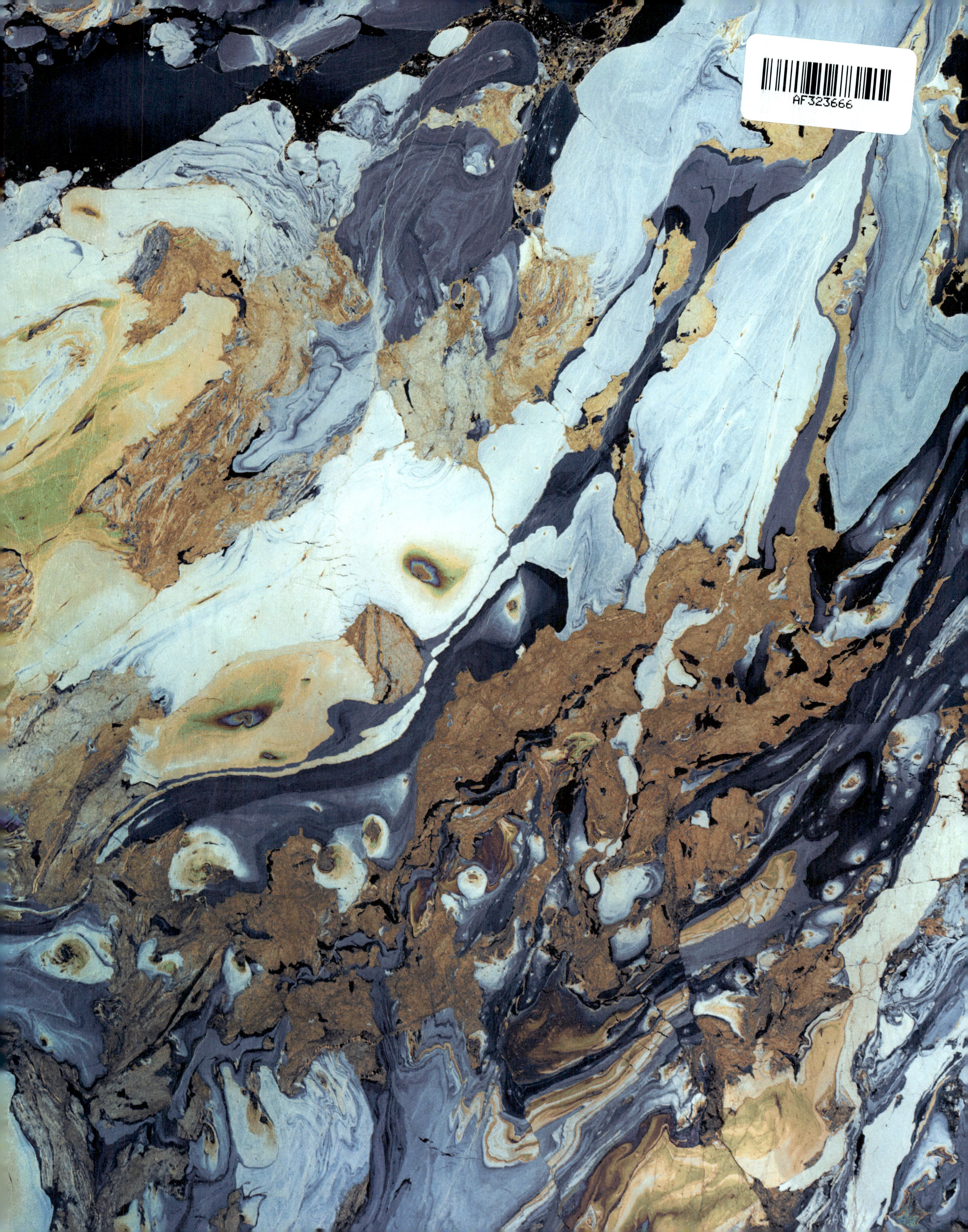

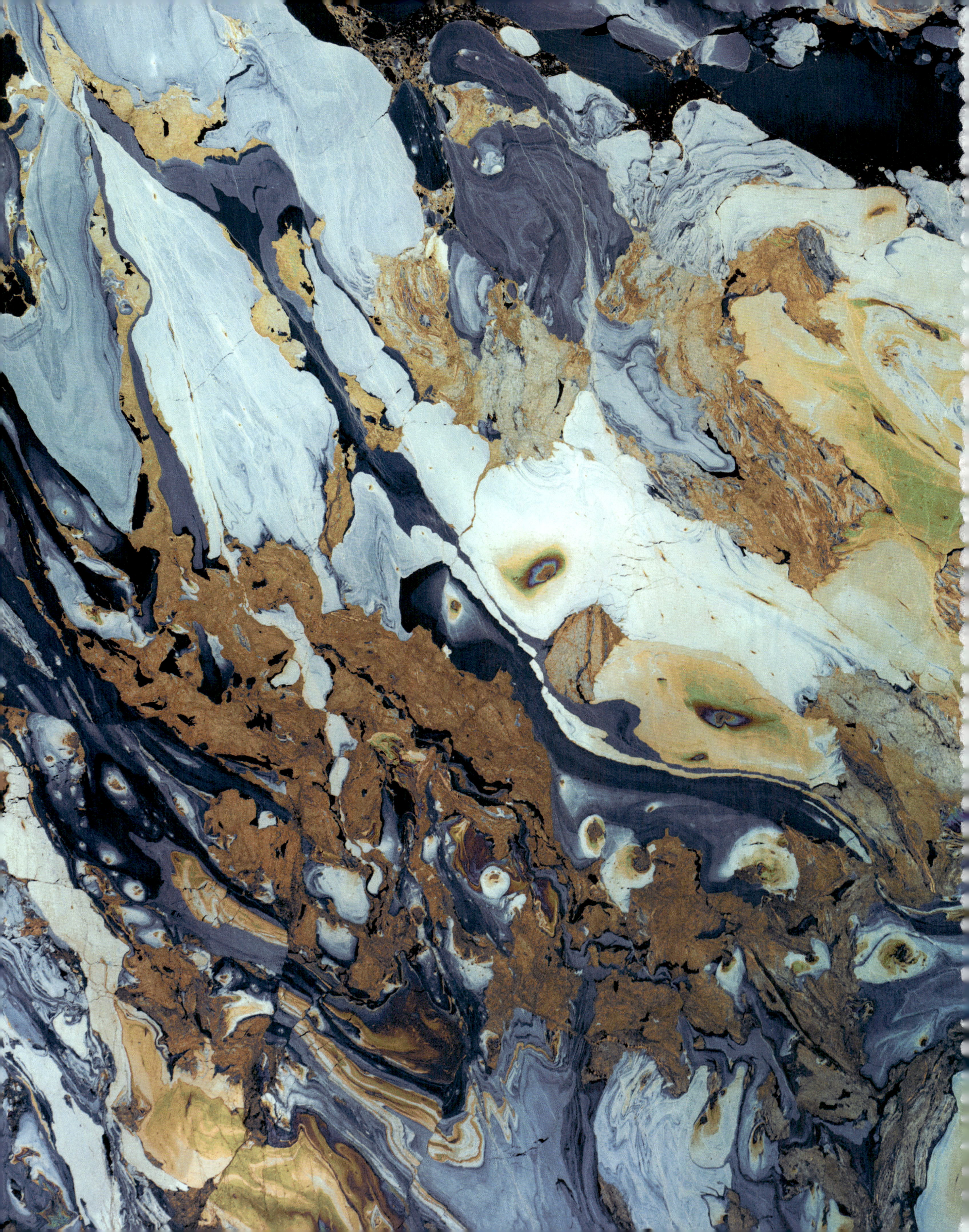

SIMEN JOHAN

POWERHOUSE BOOKS. BROOKLYN, NY

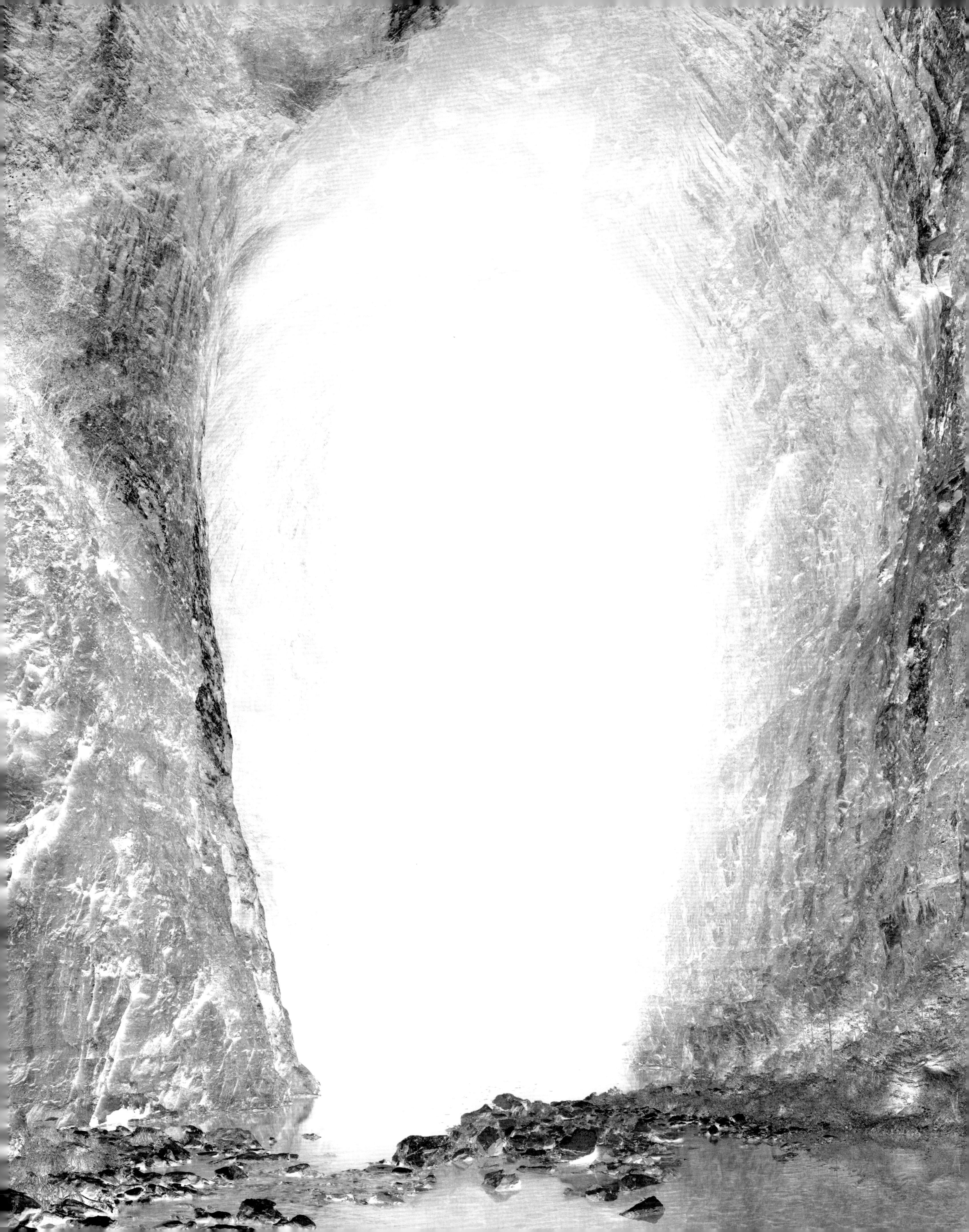

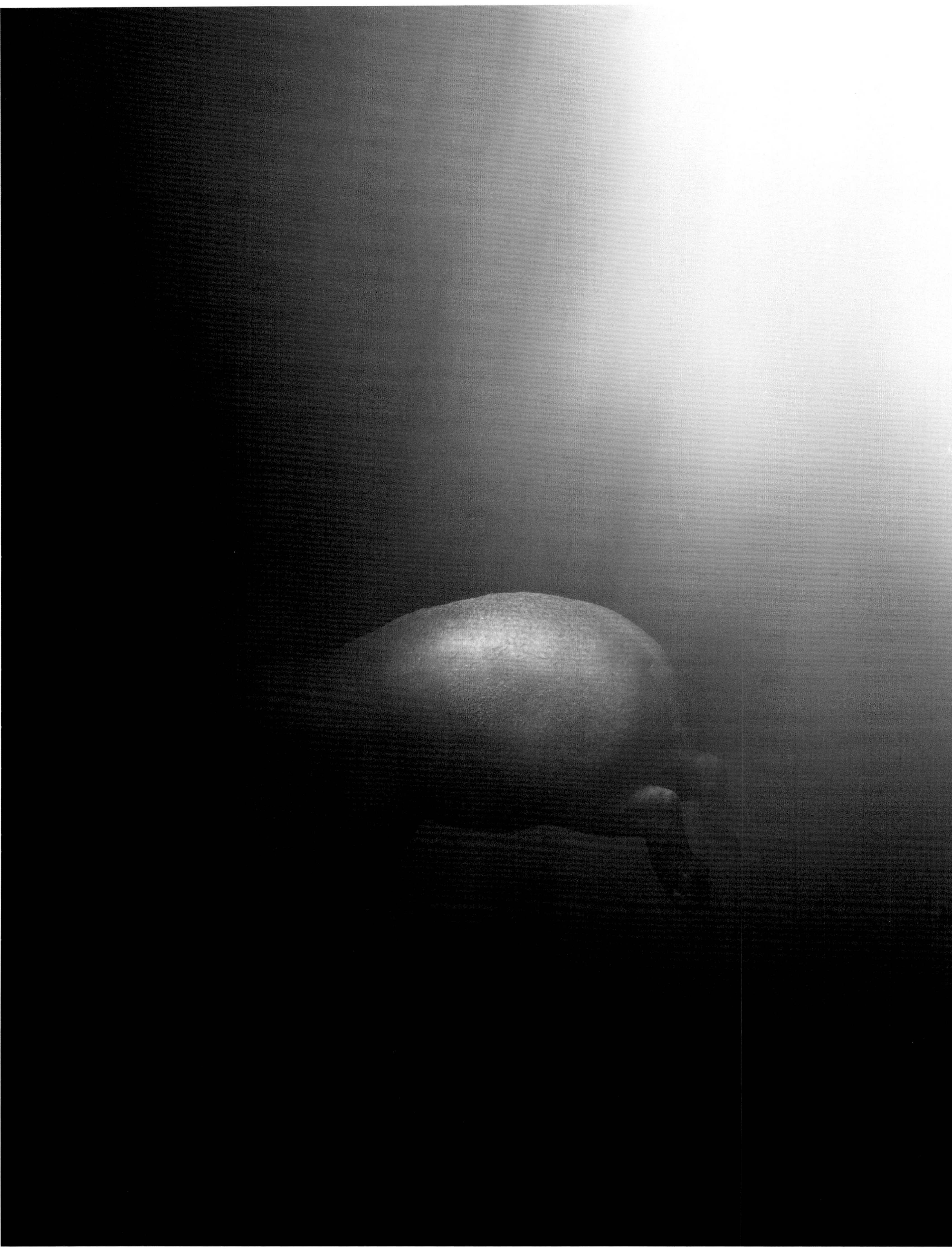

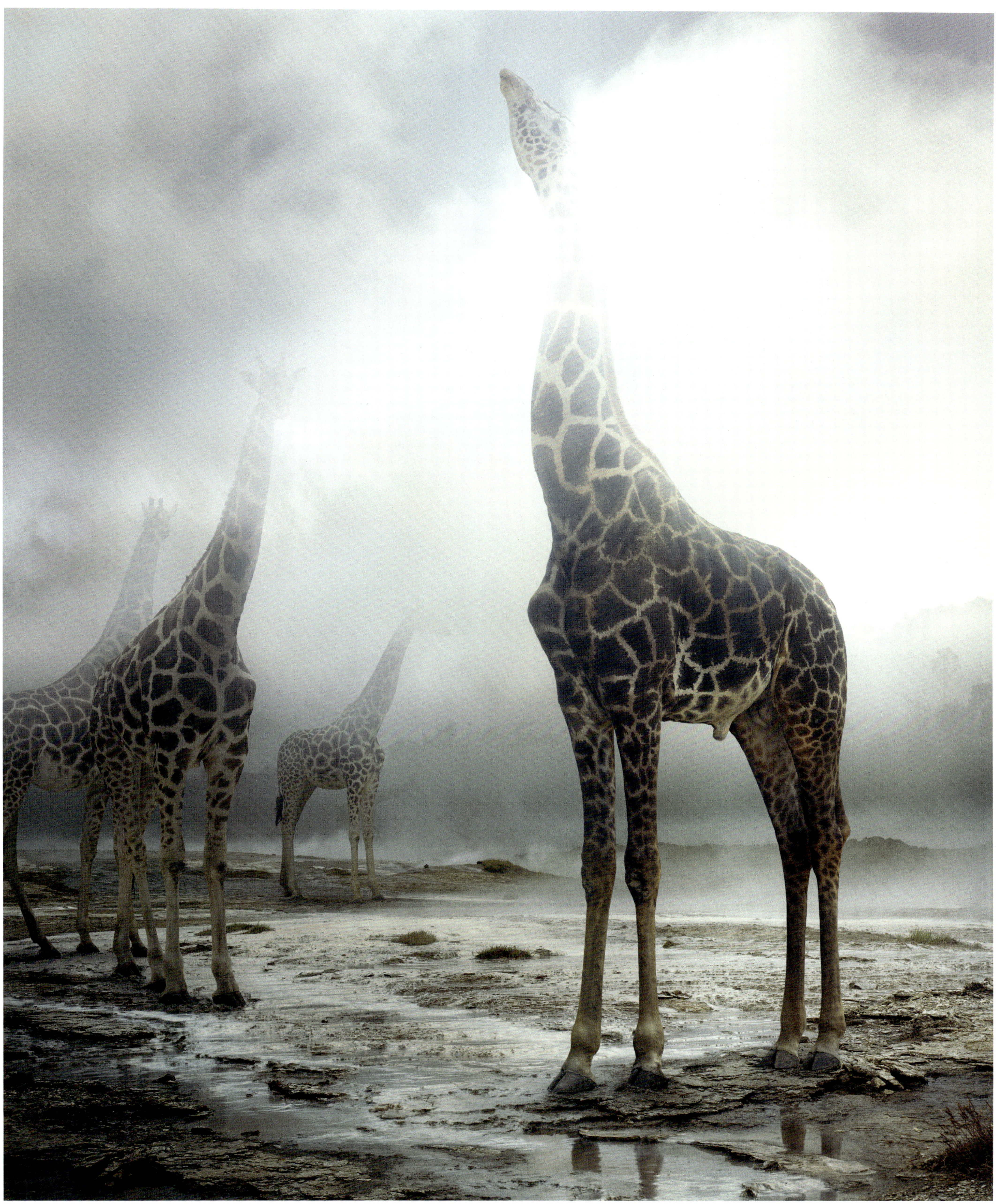

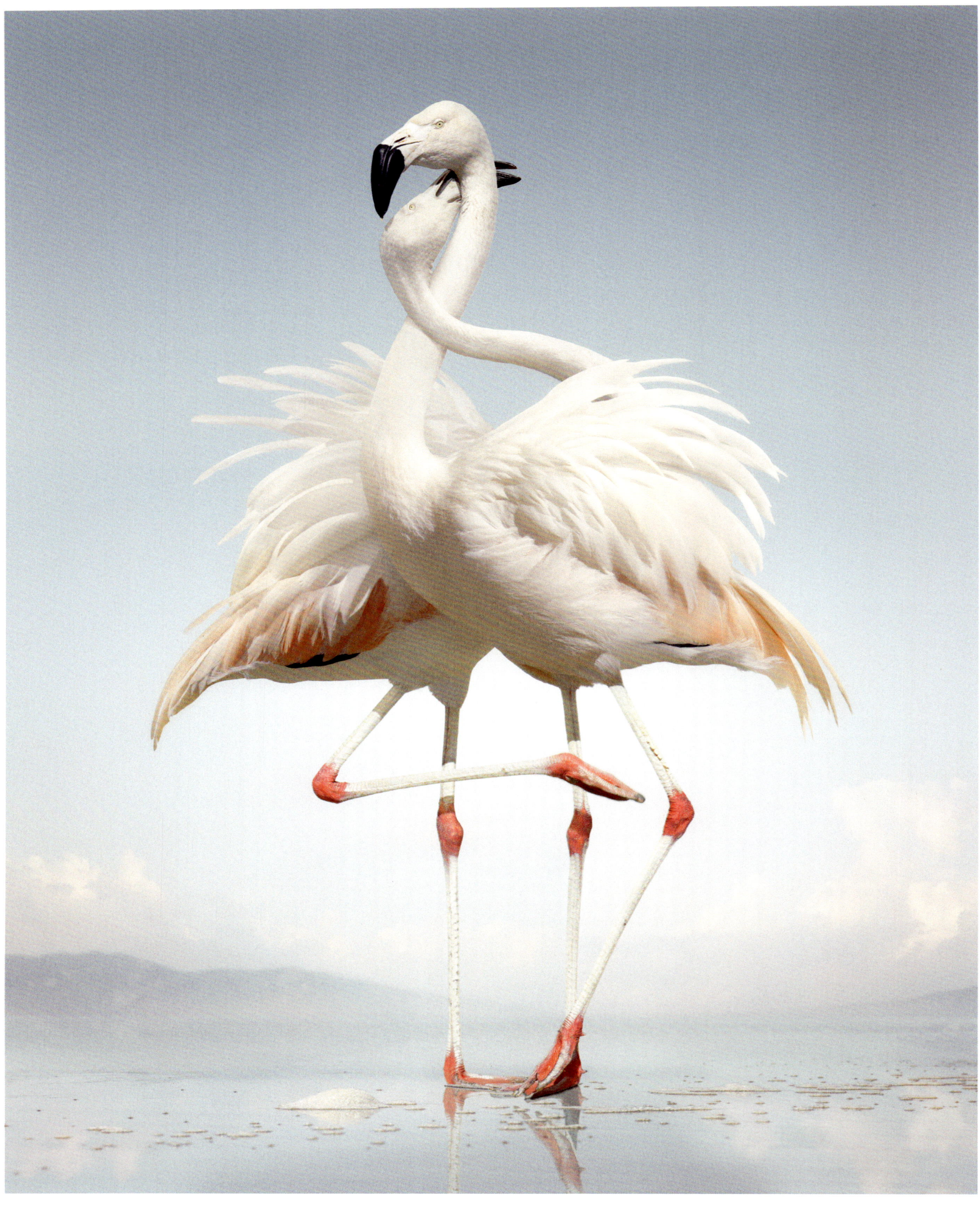

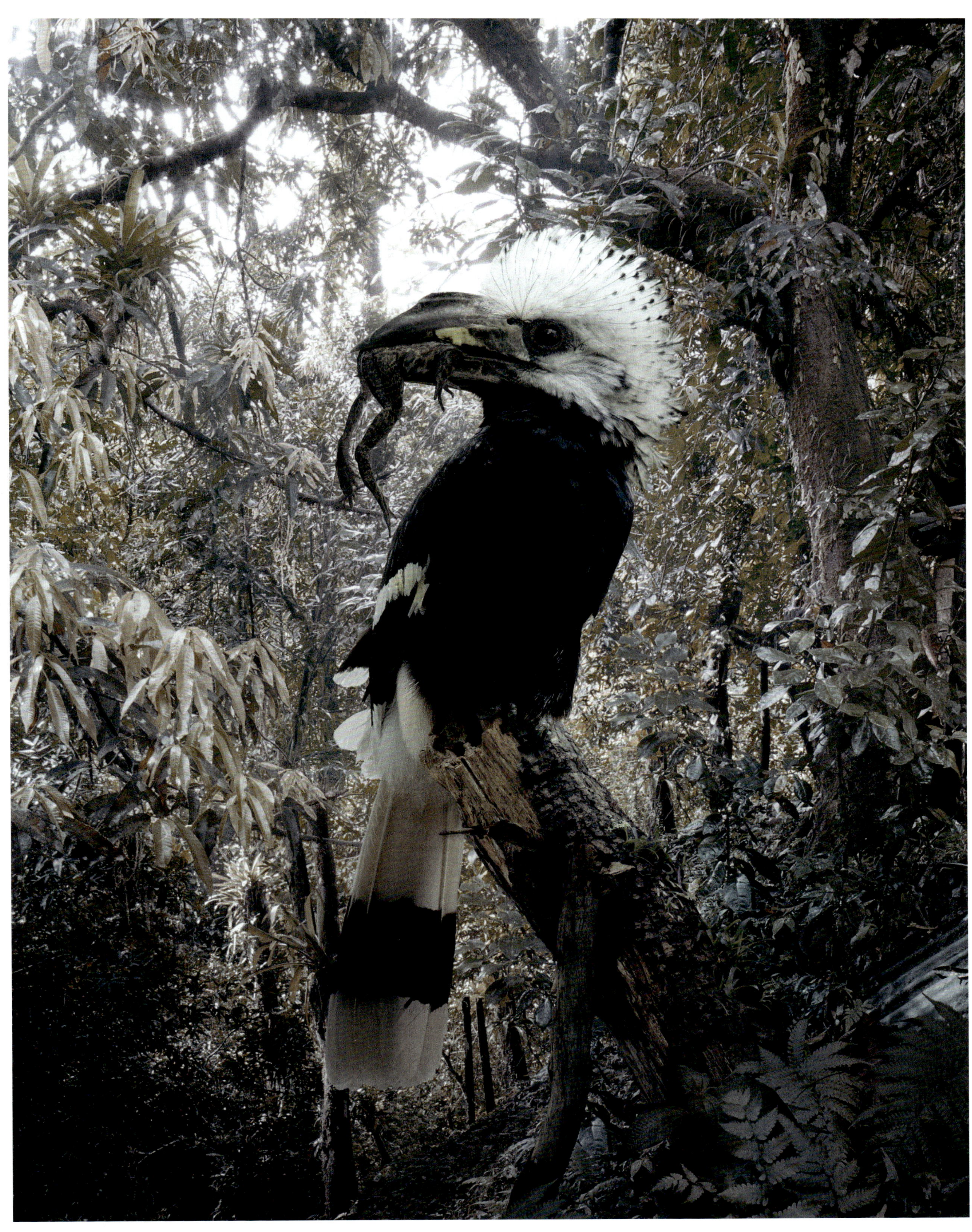

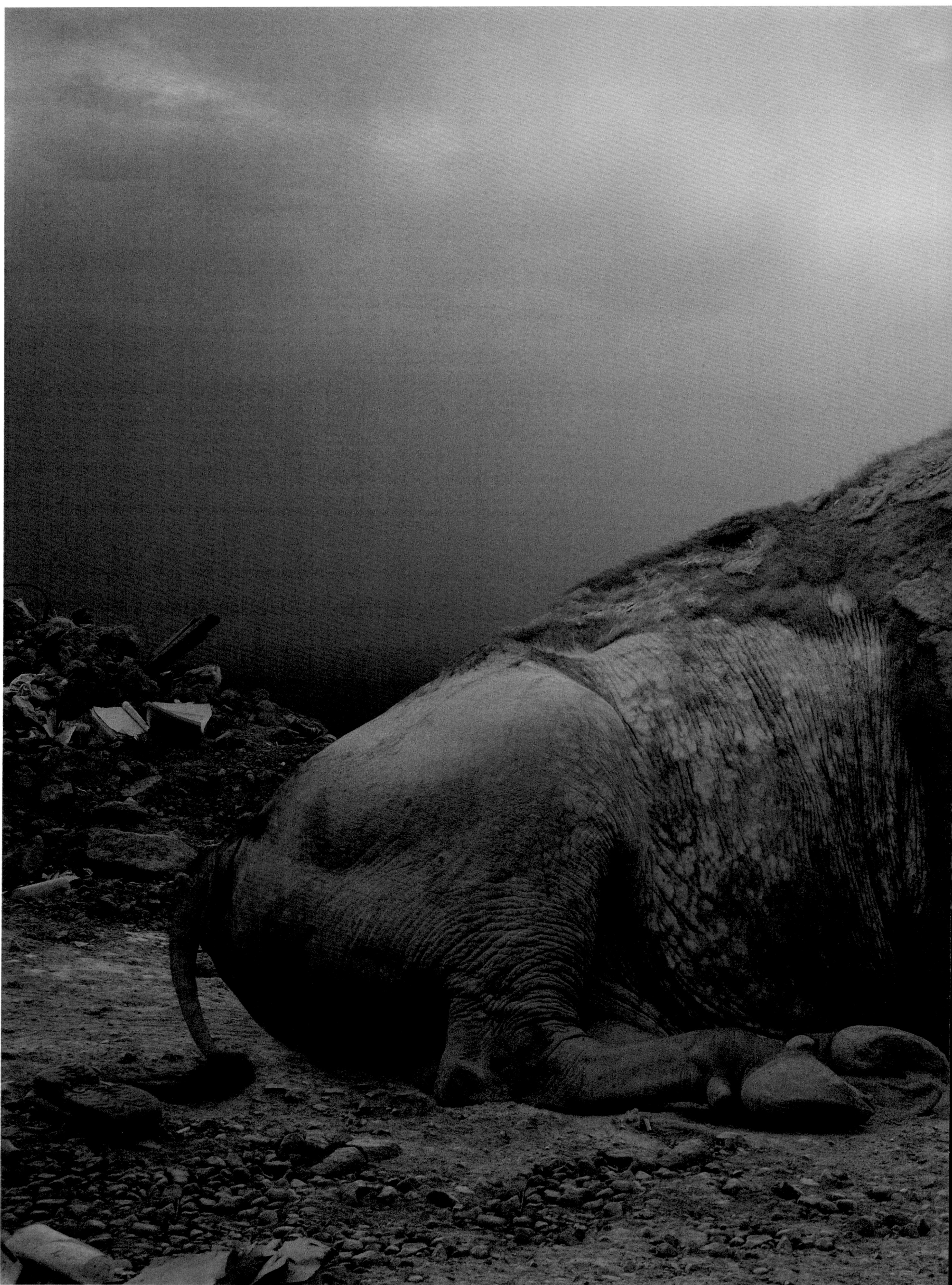

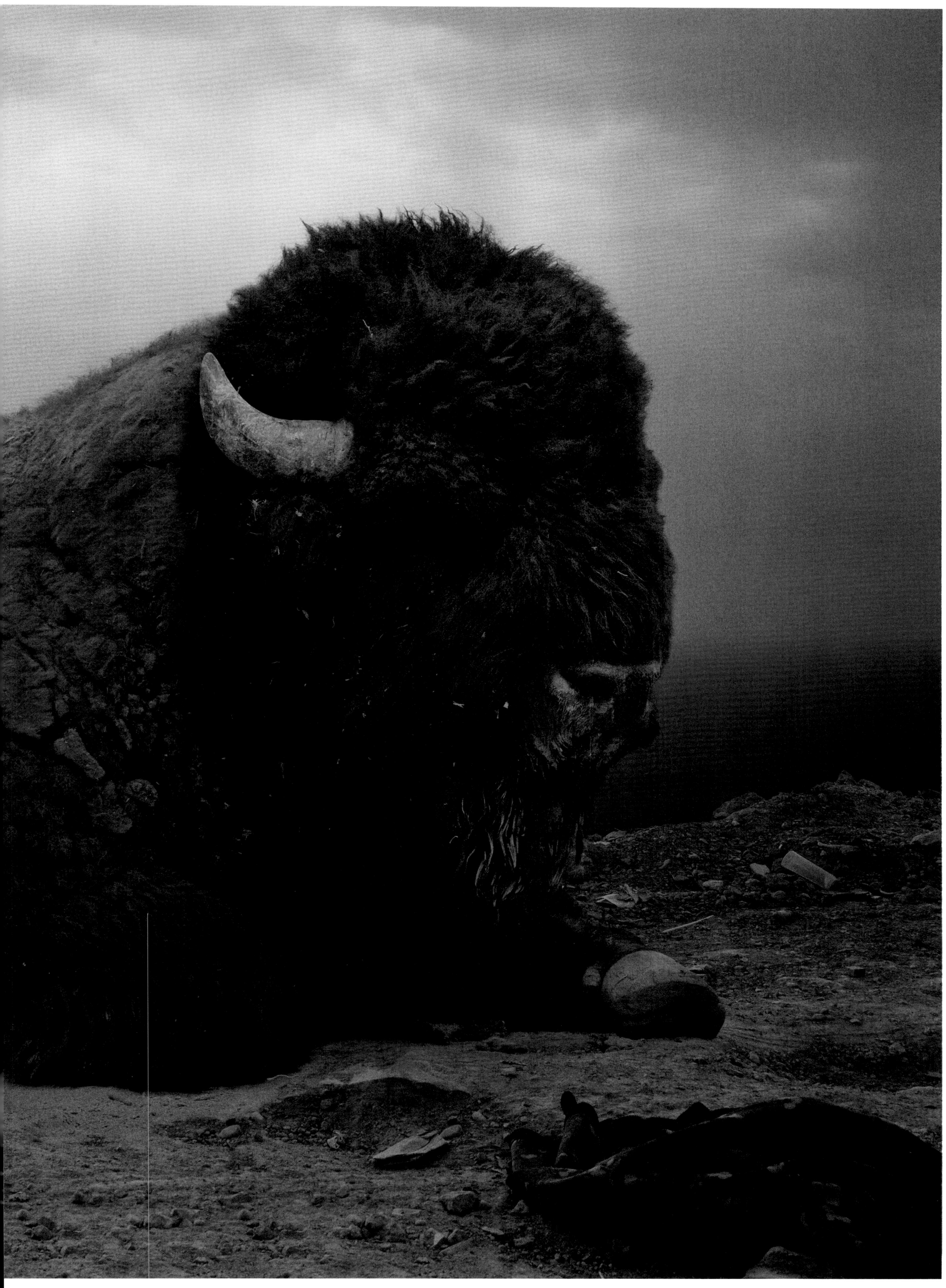

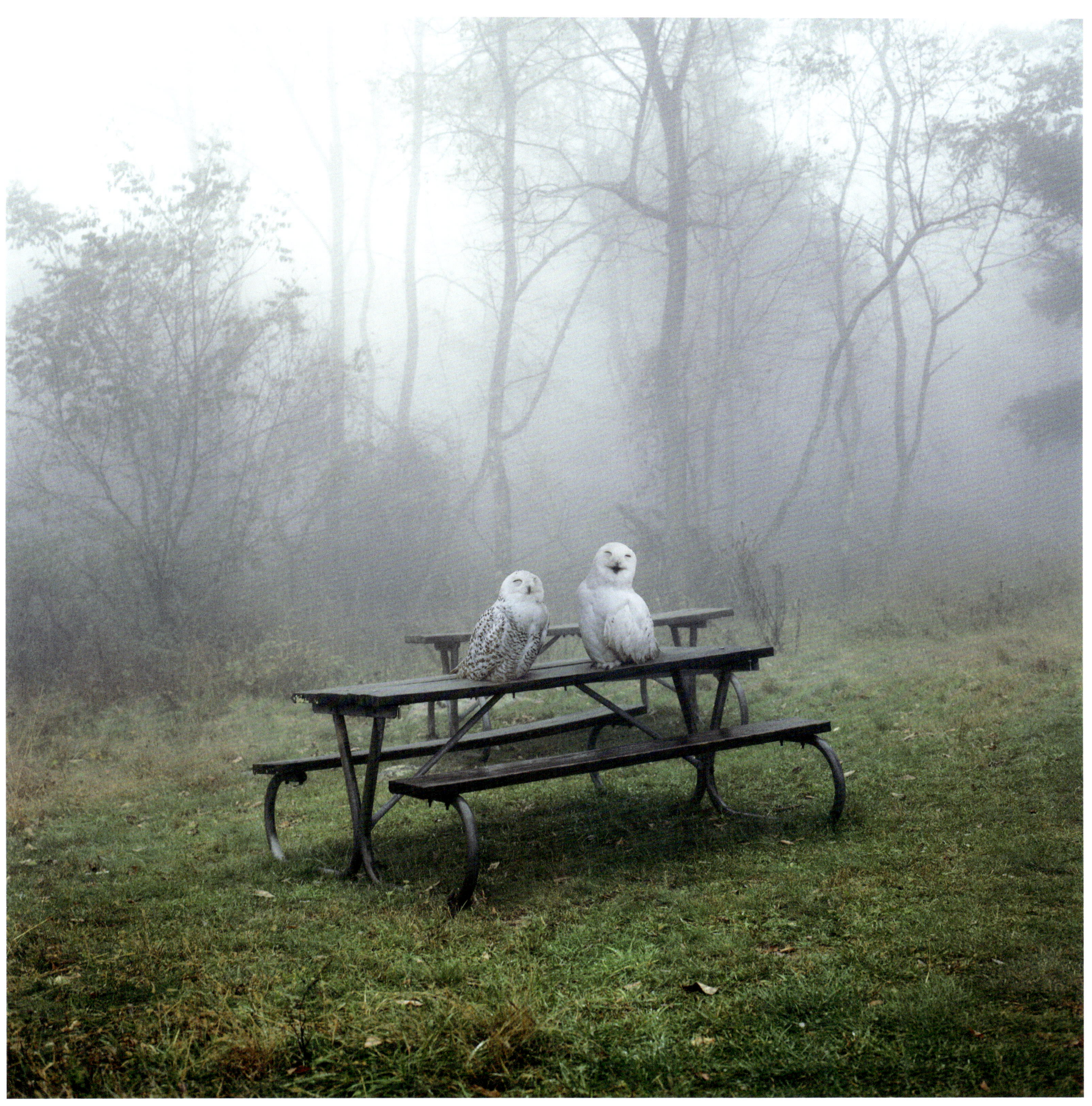

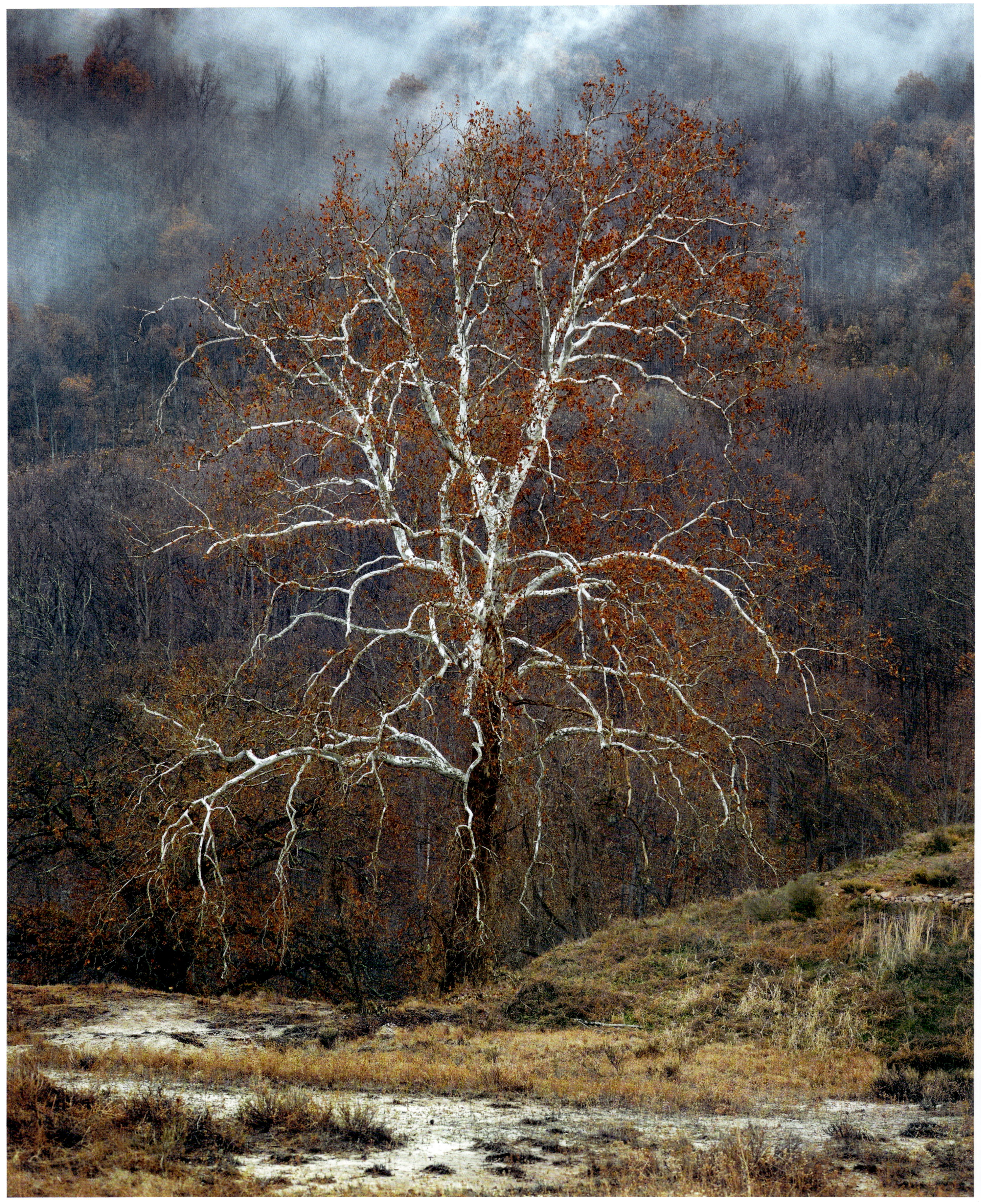

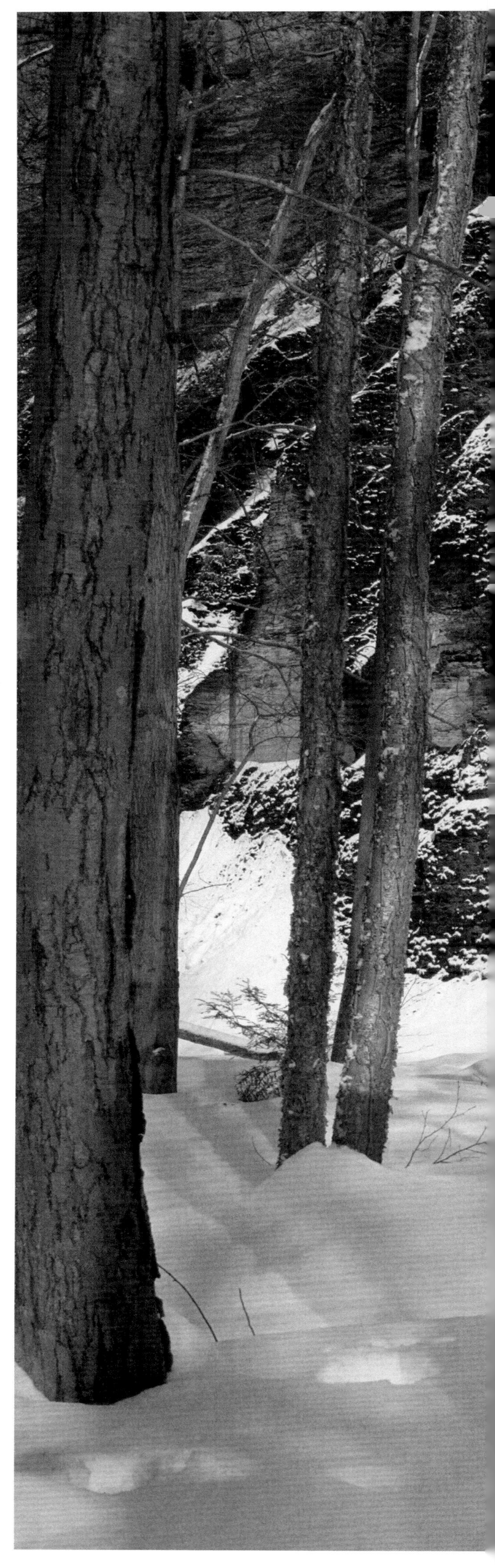

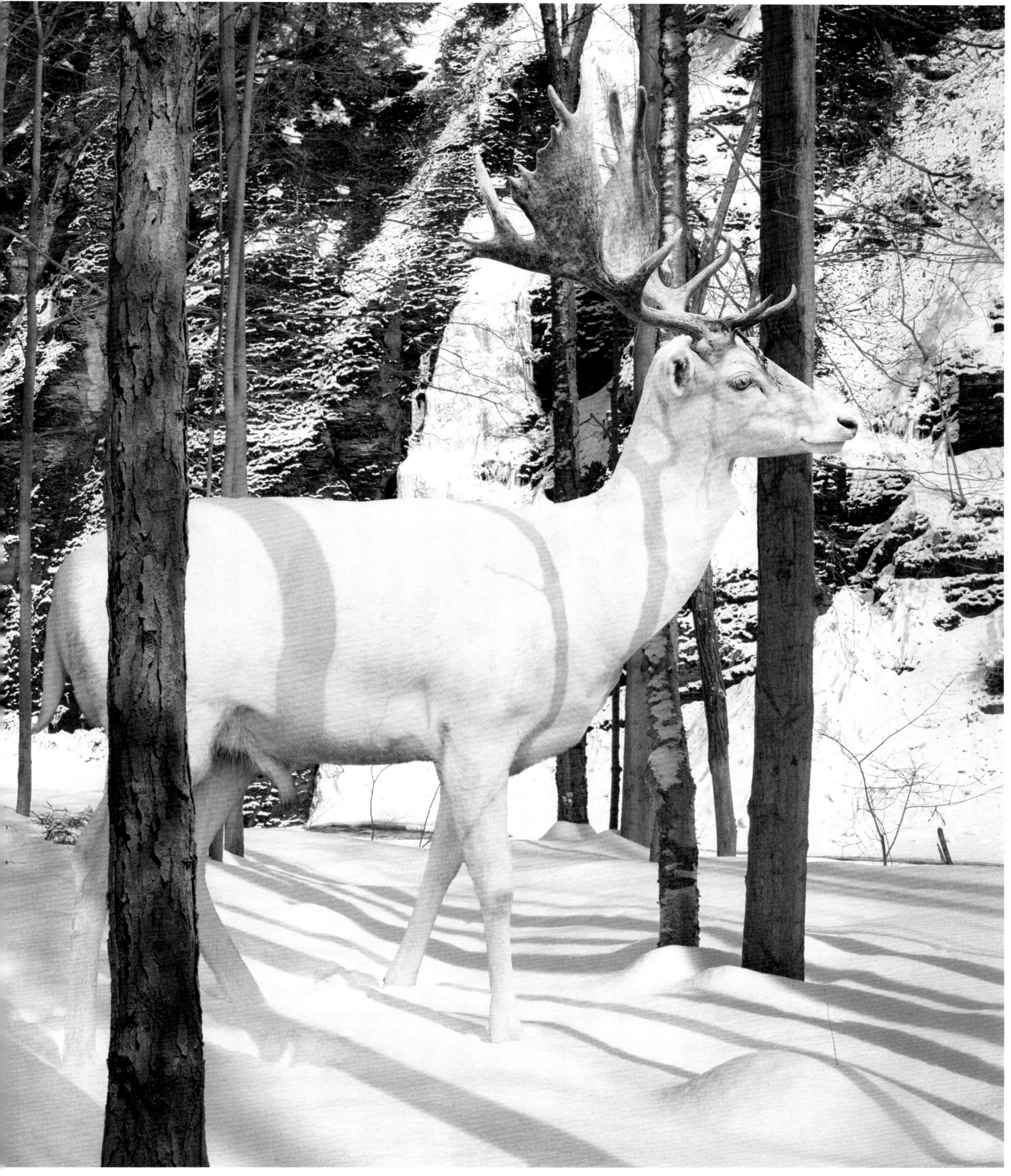

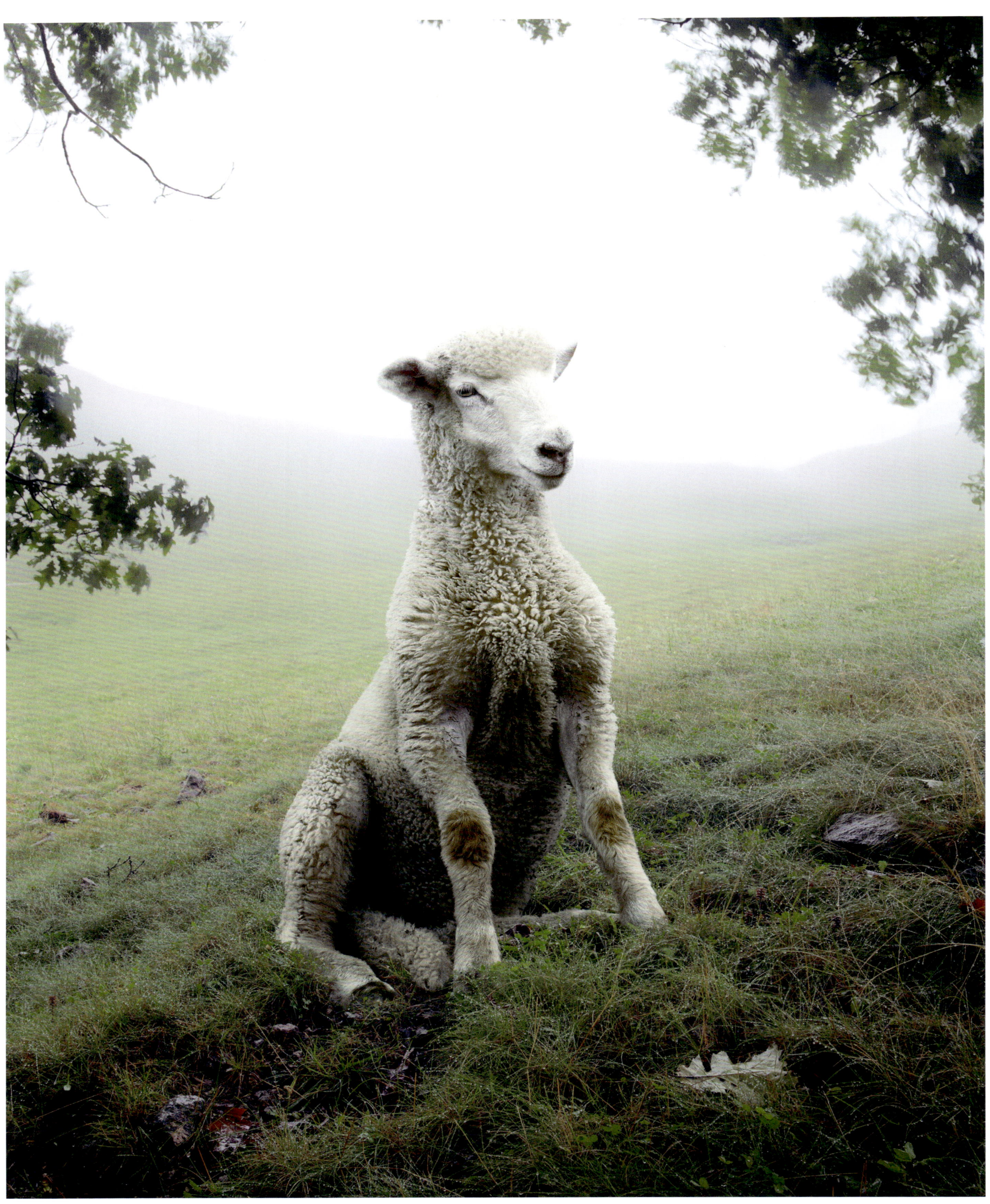

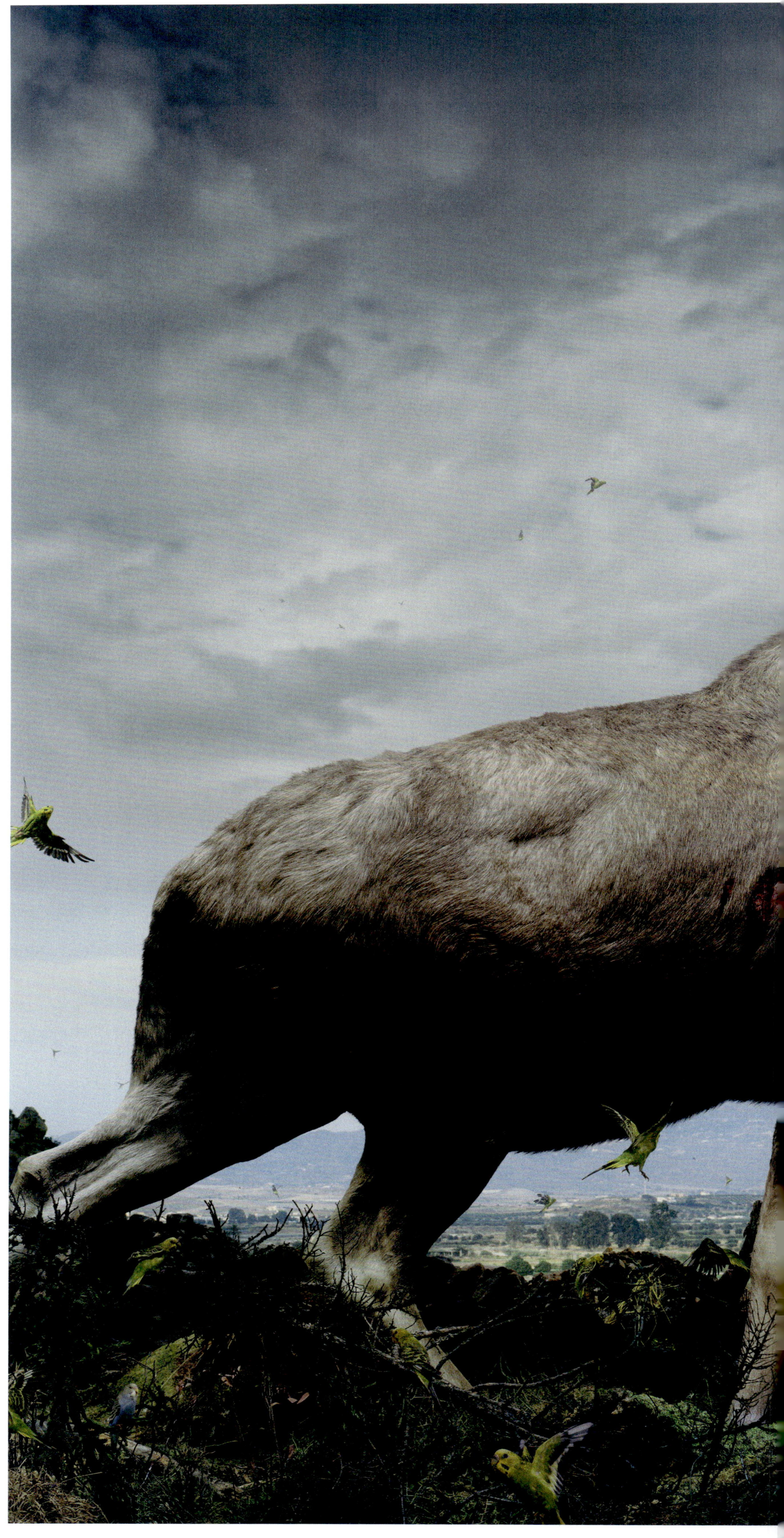

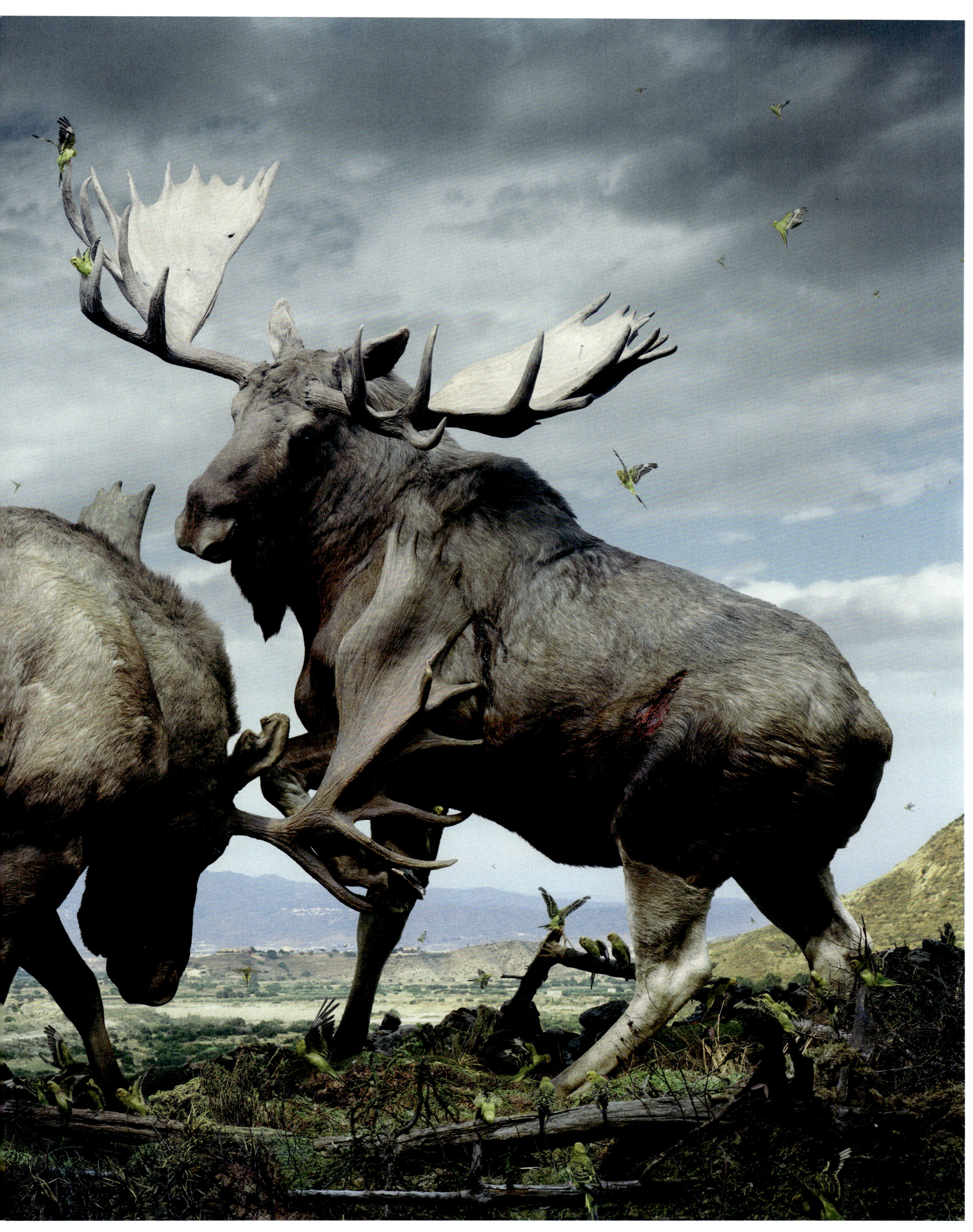

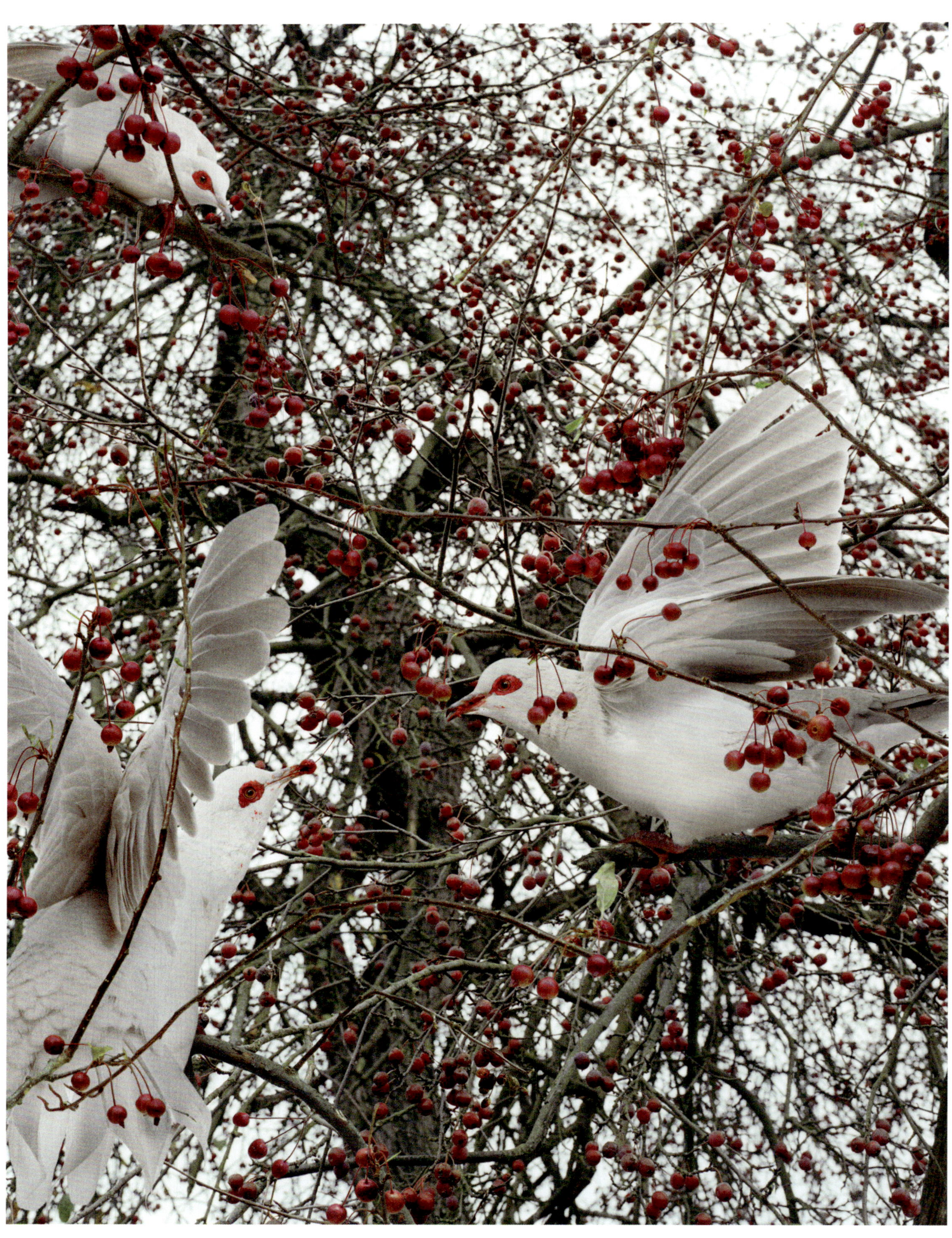

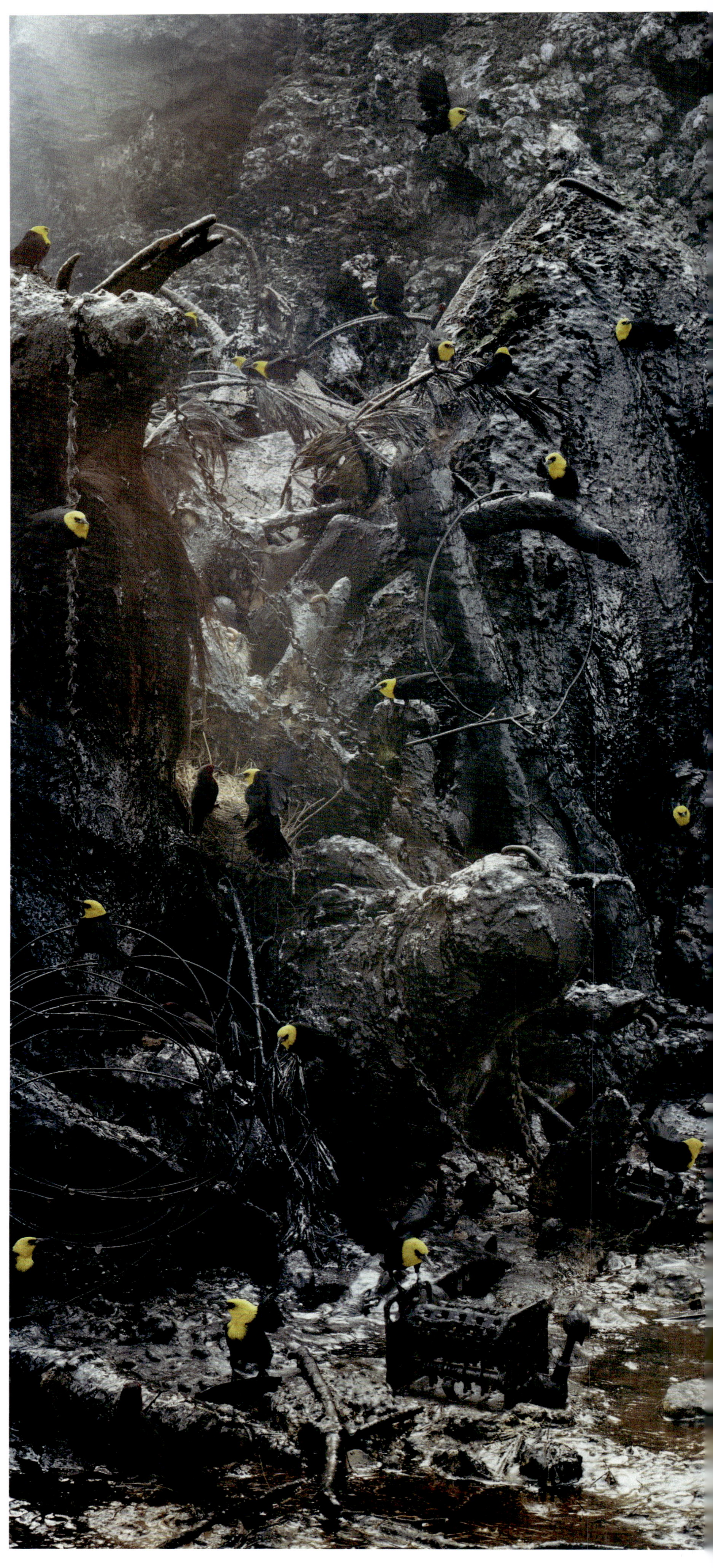

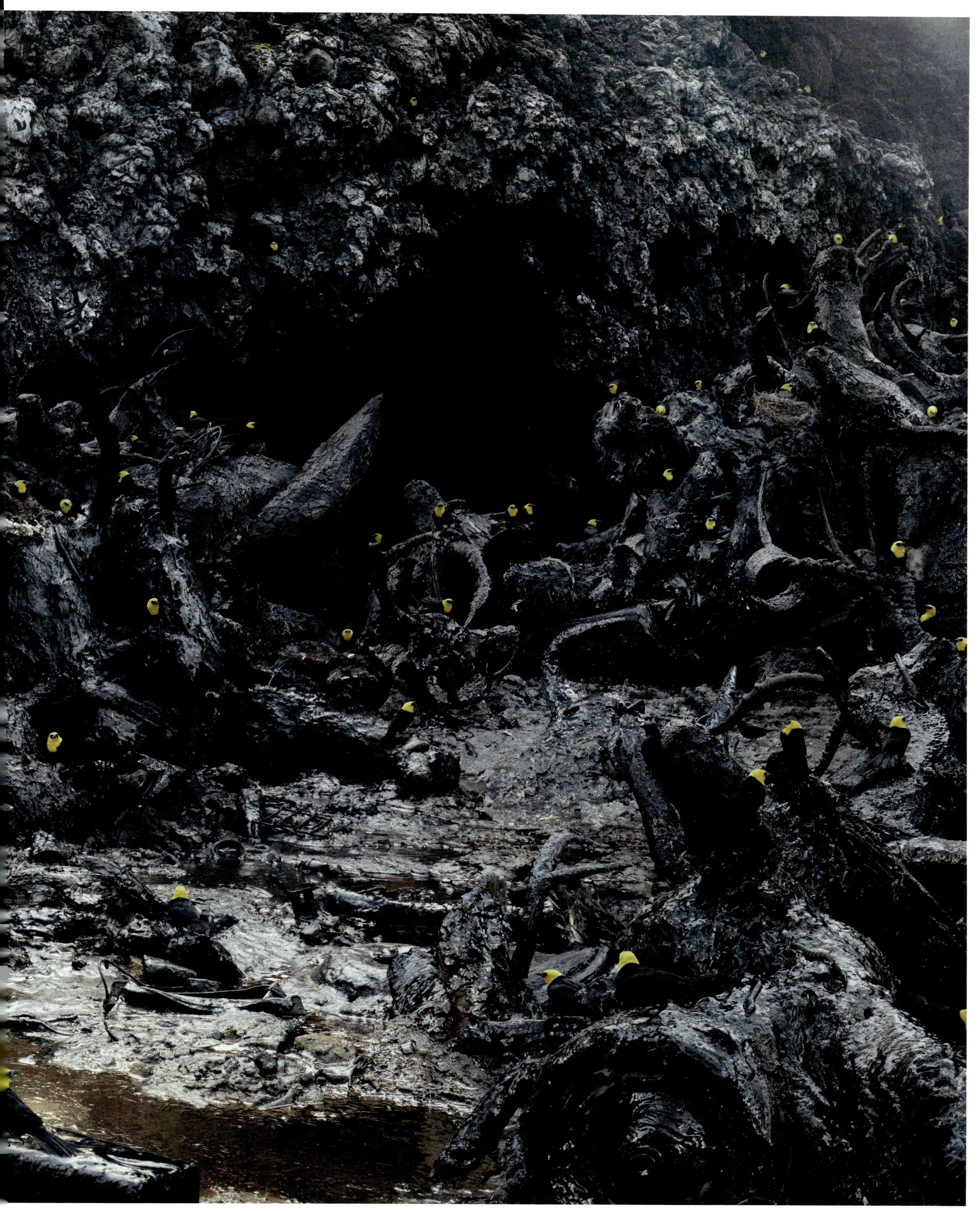

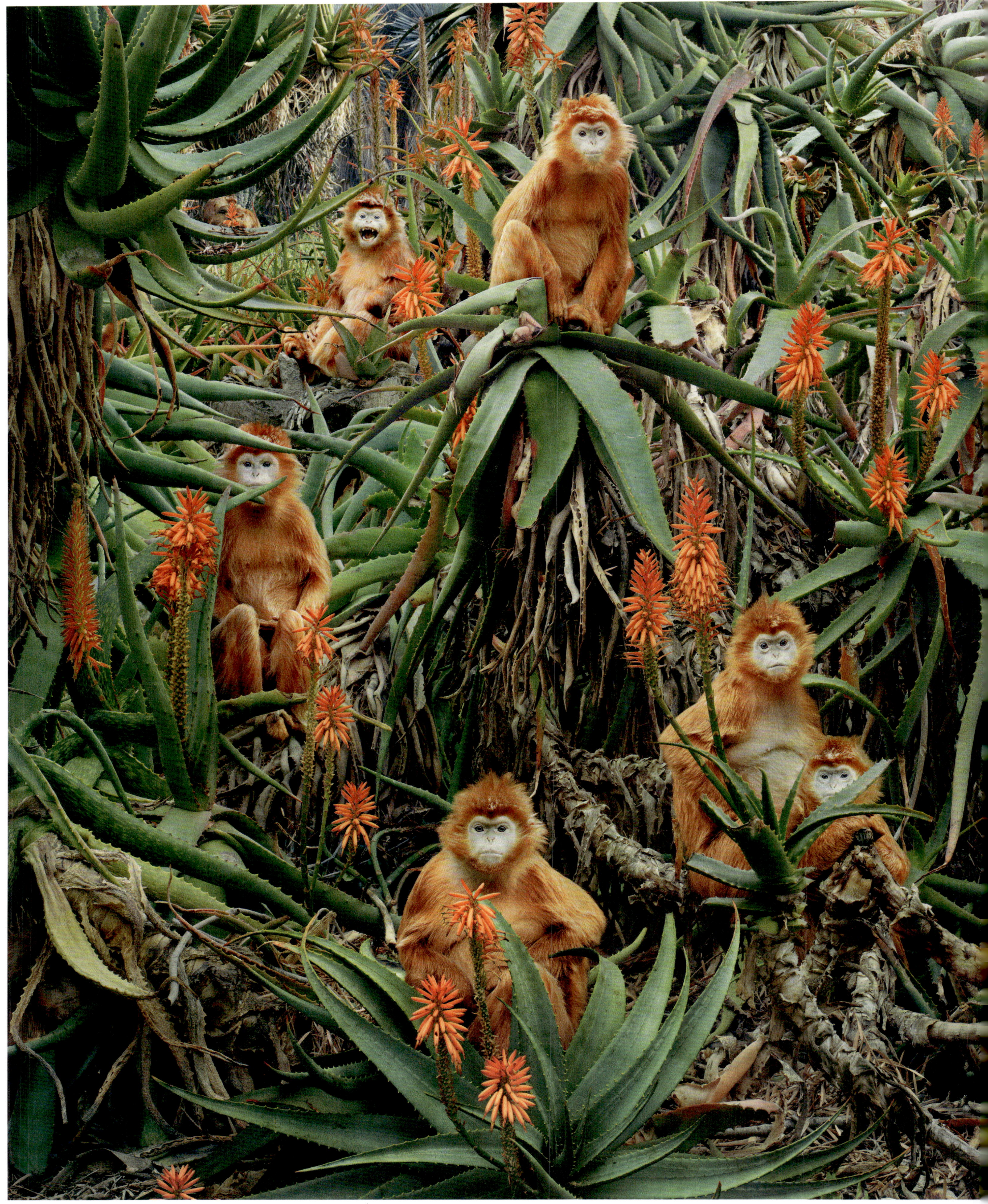

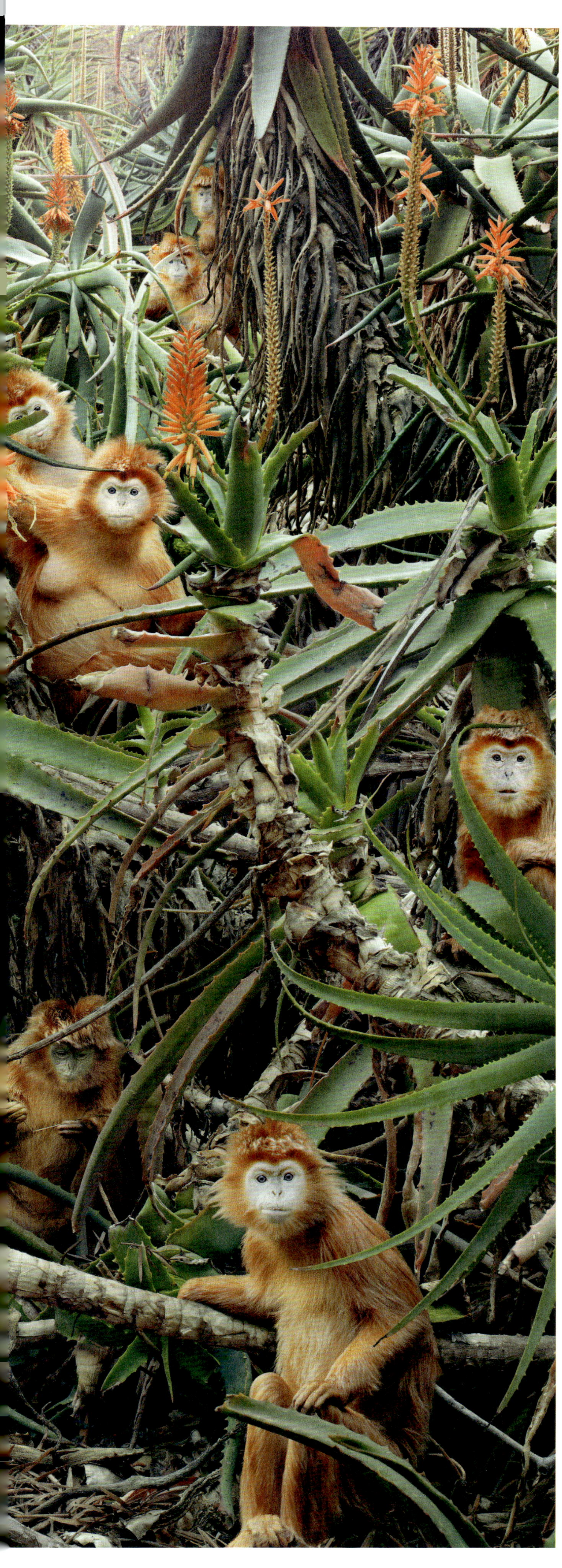

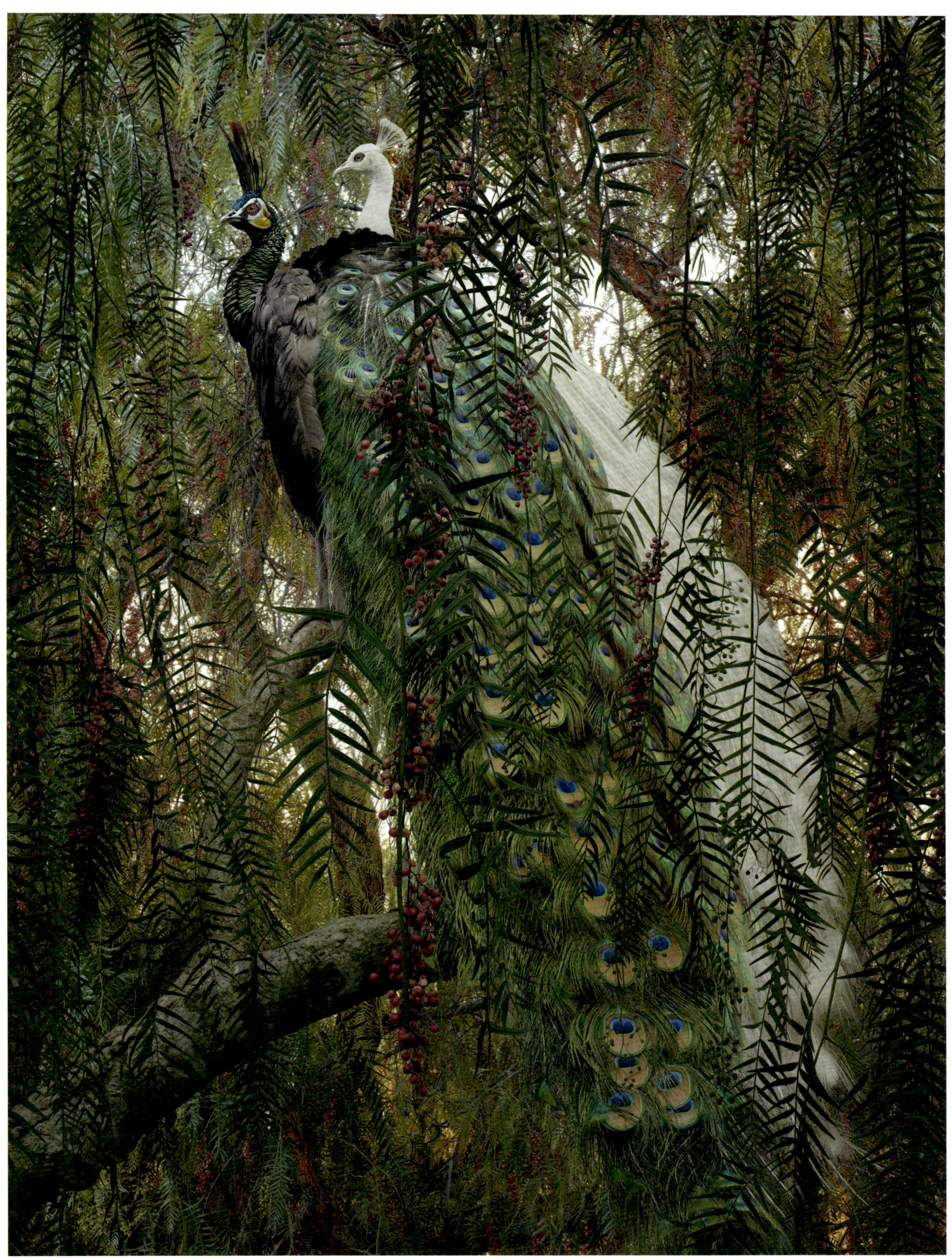

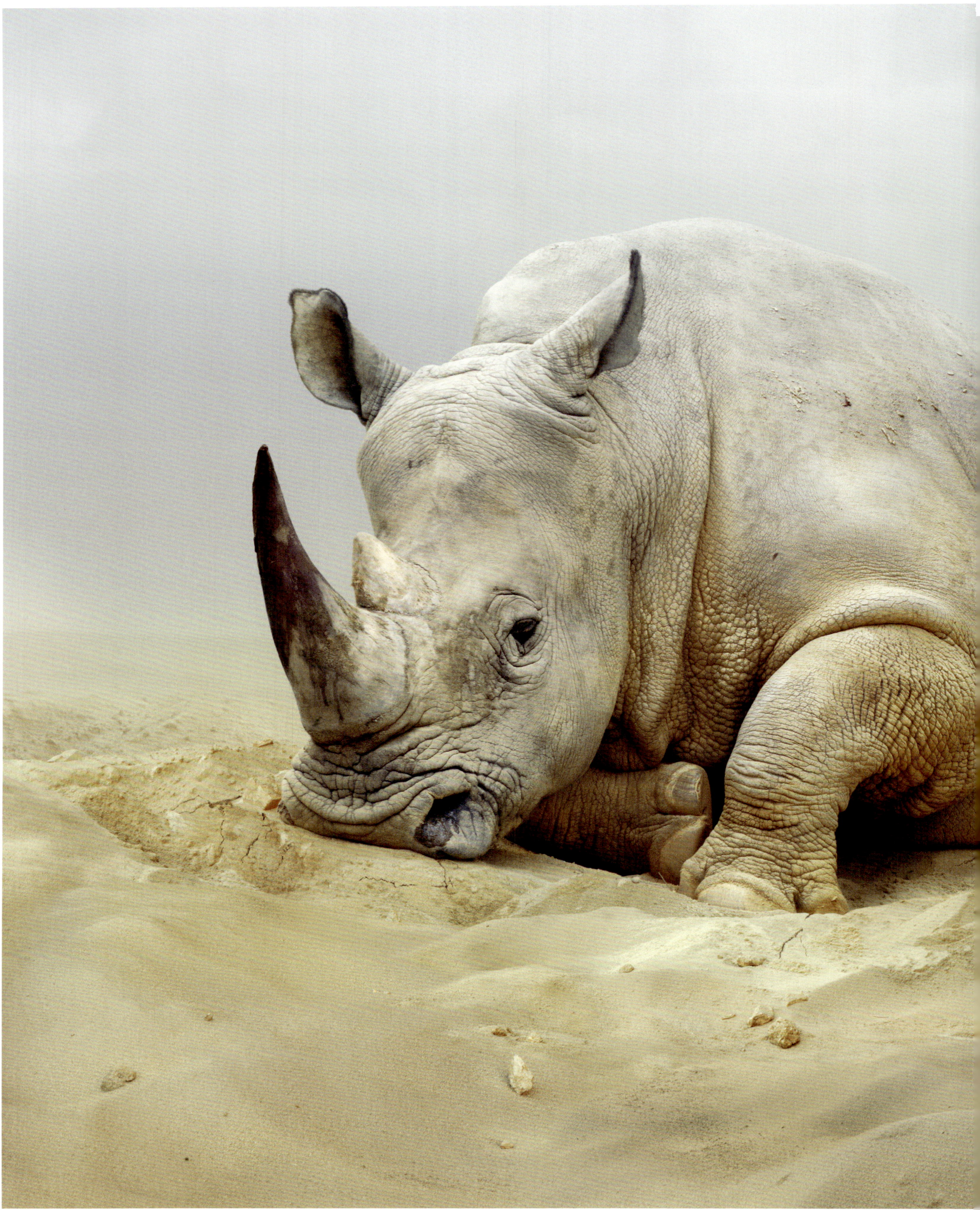

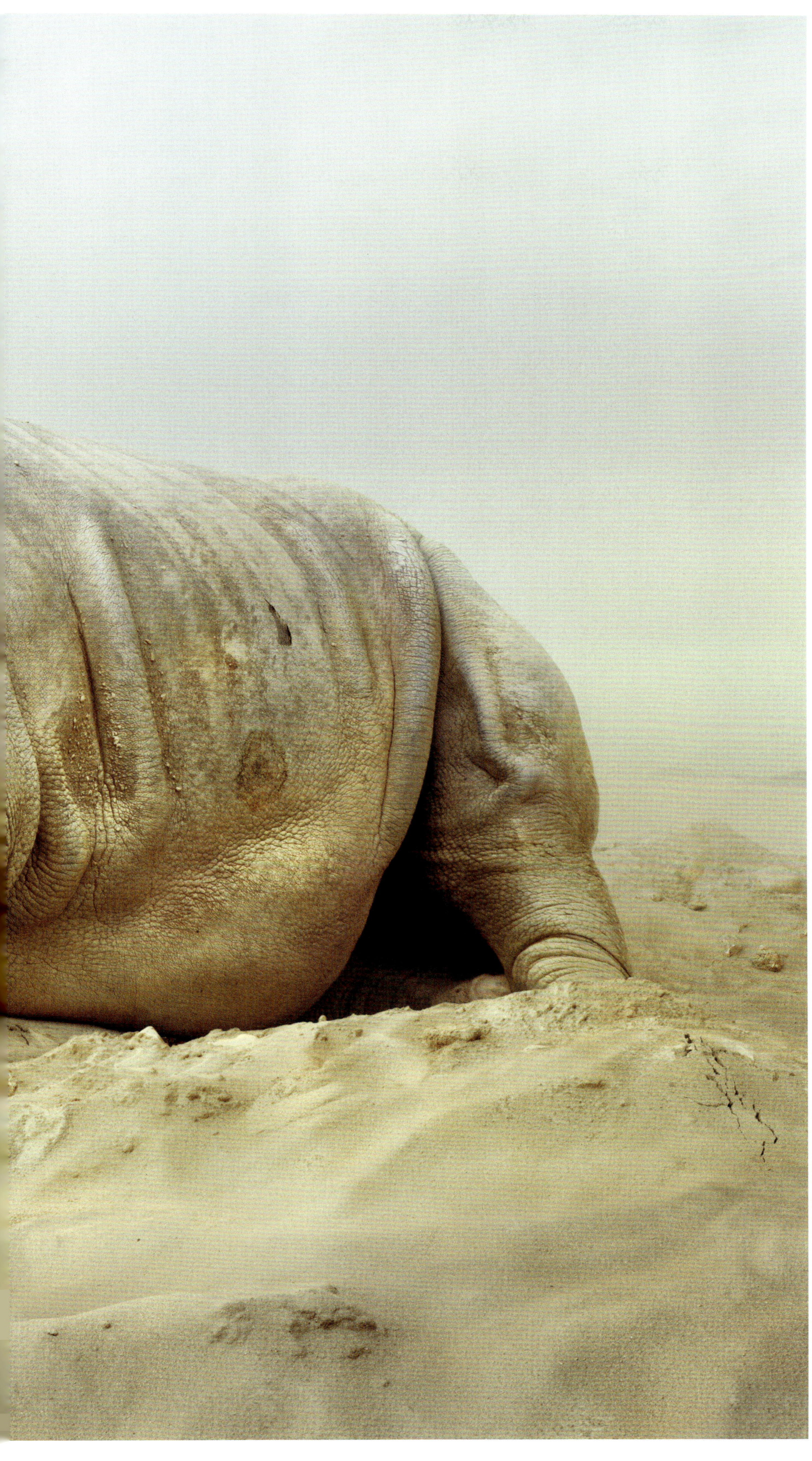

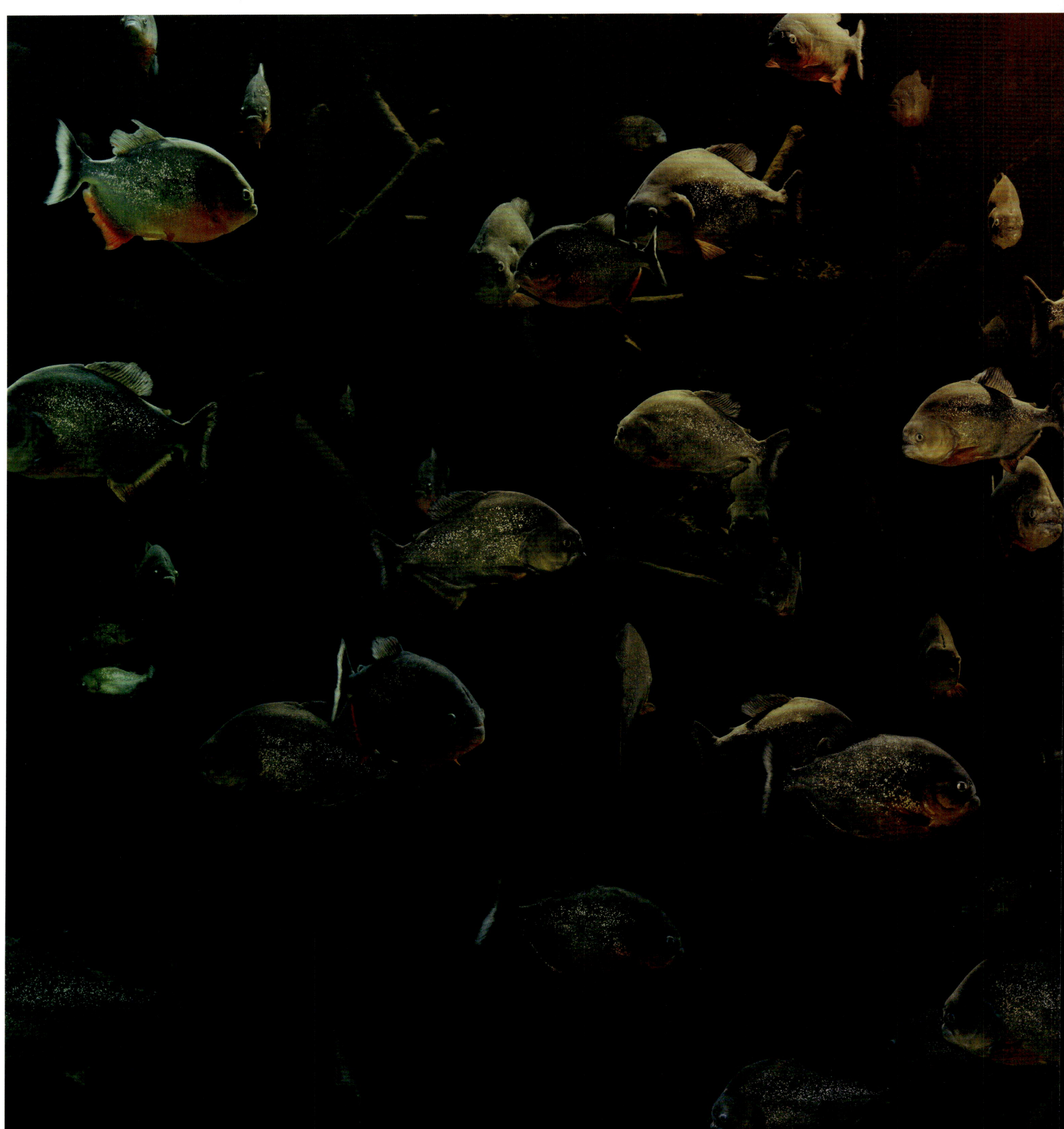

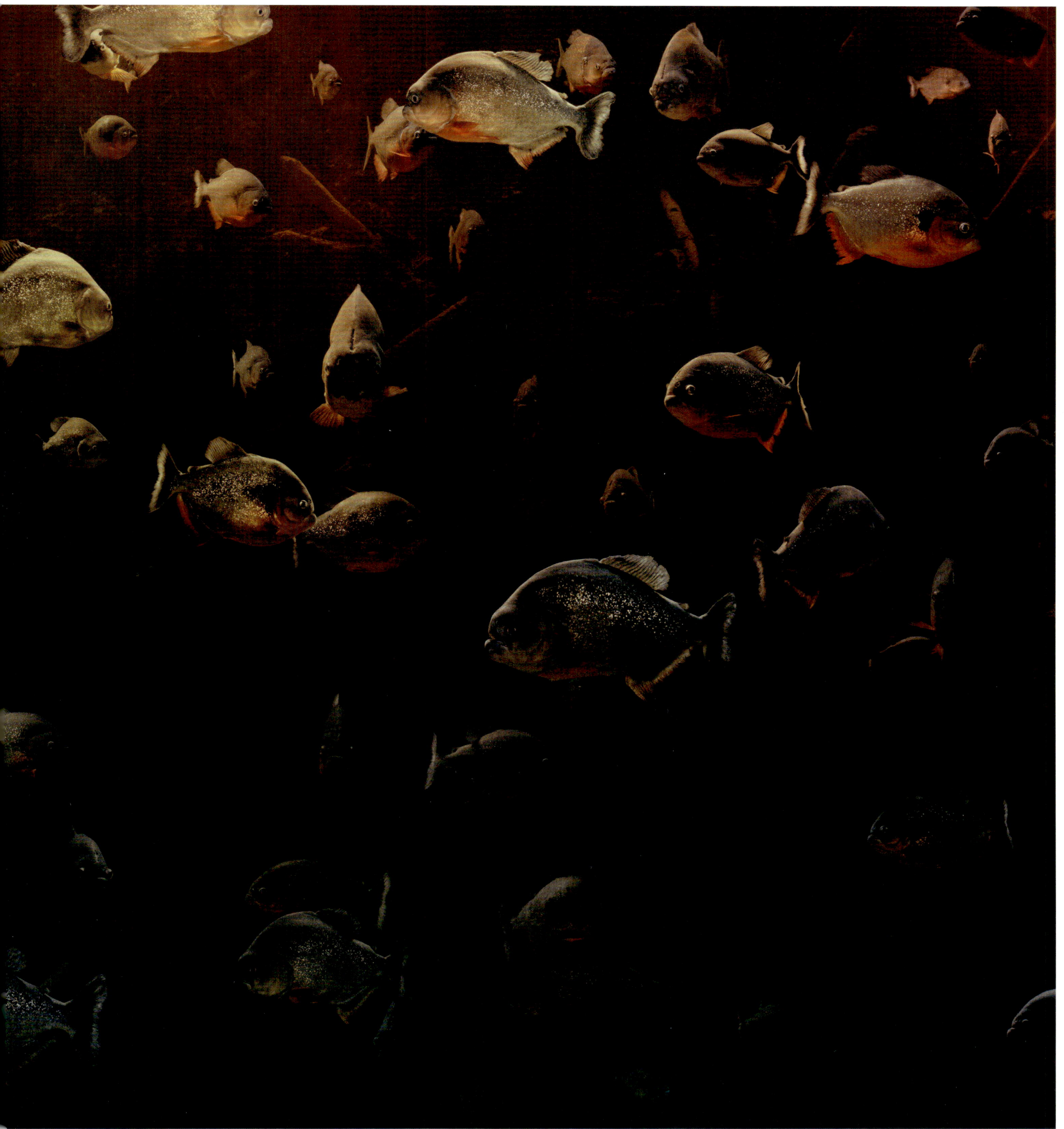

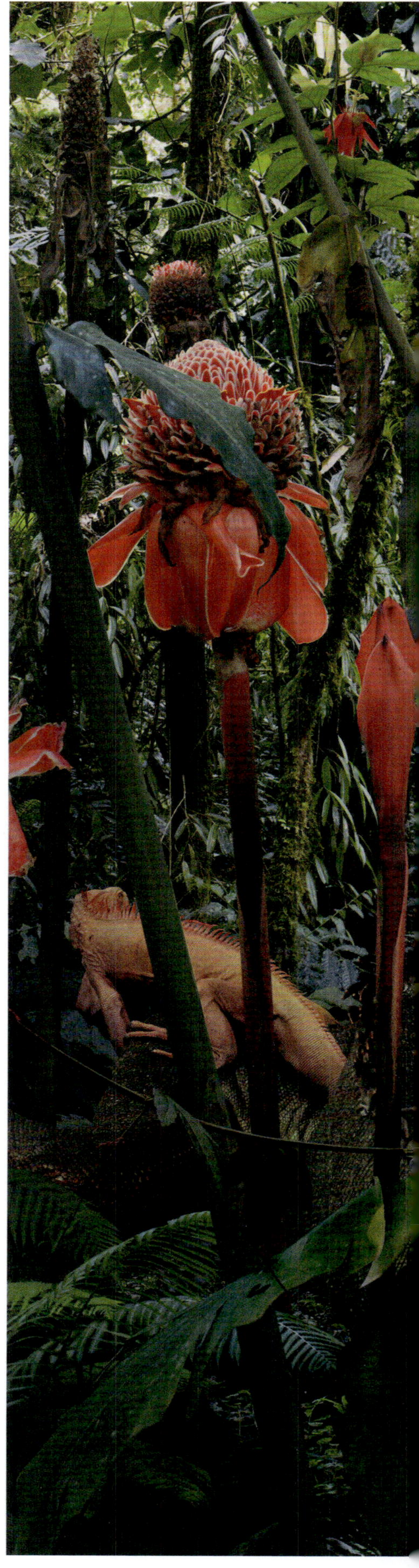

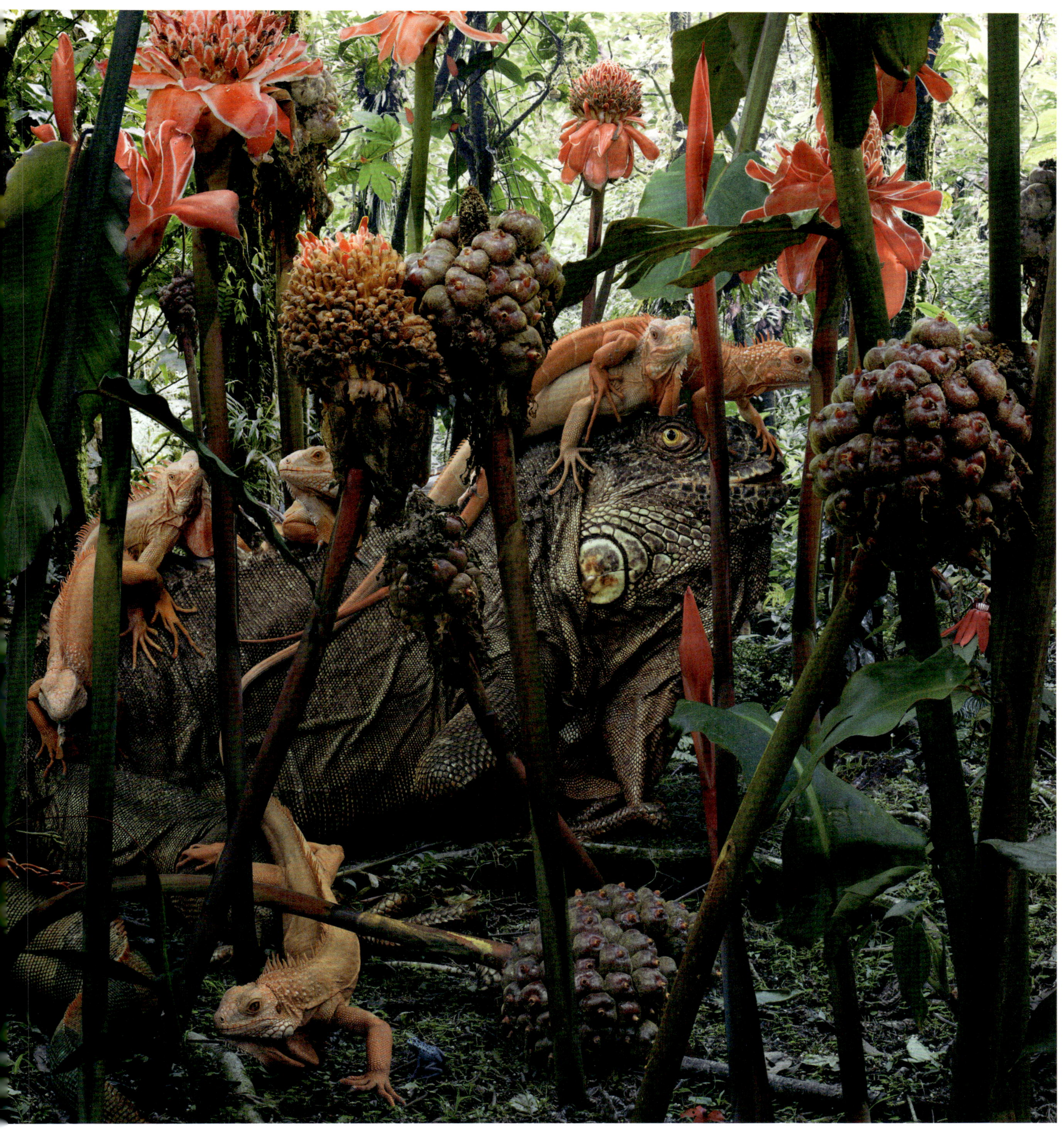

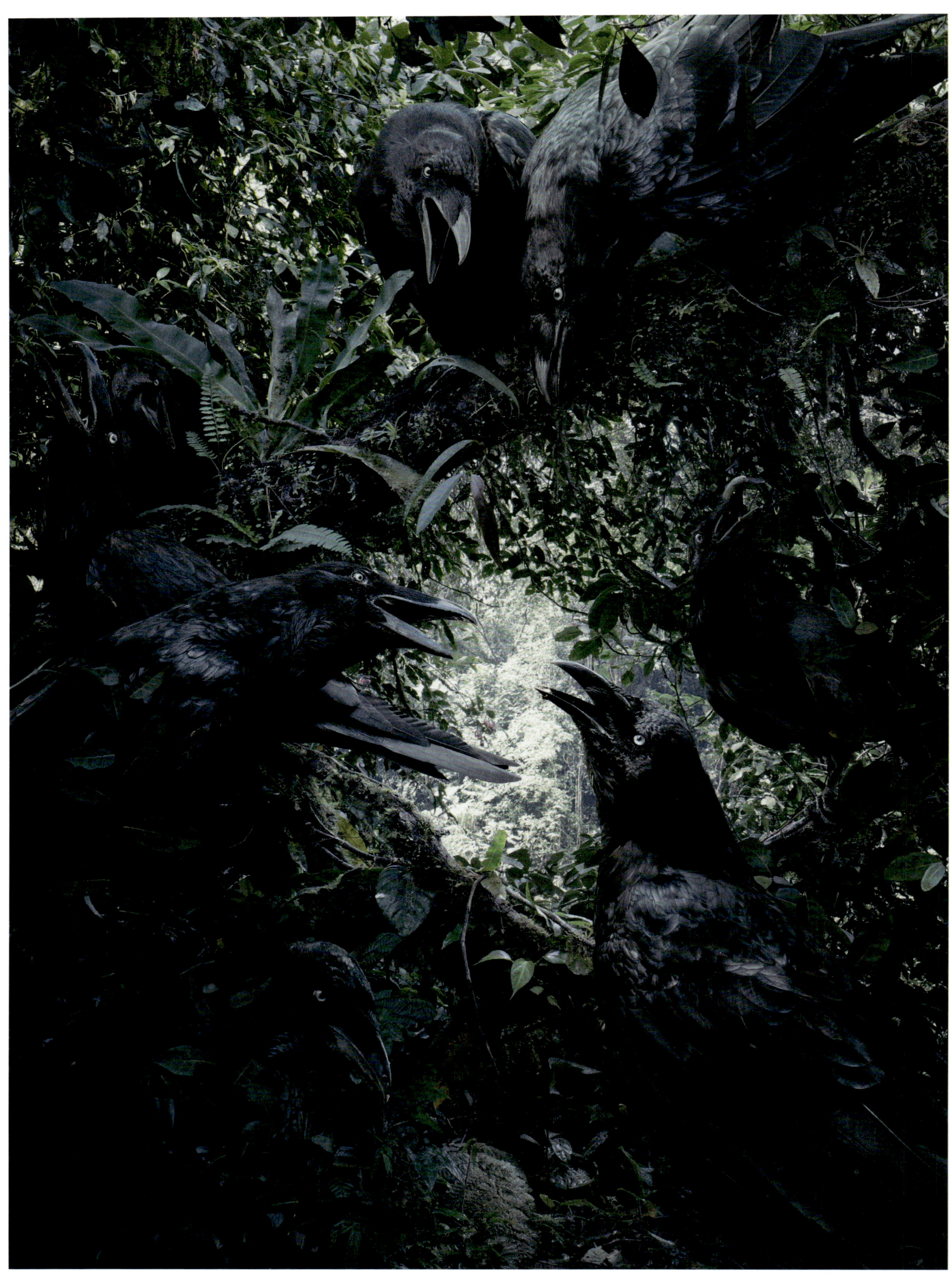

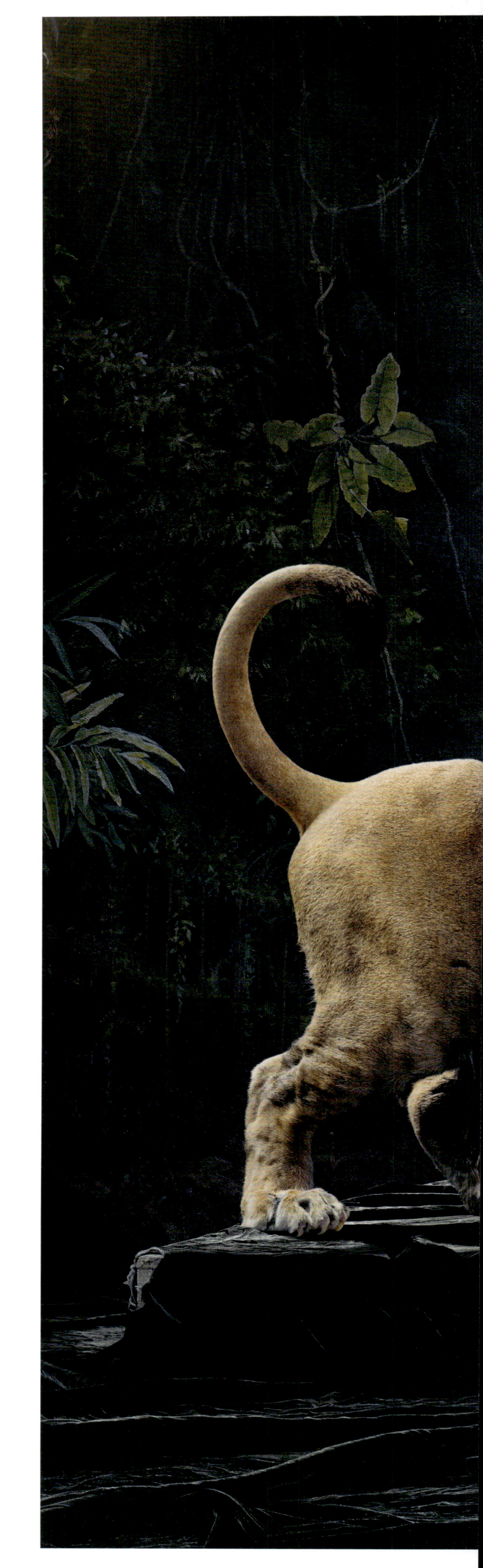

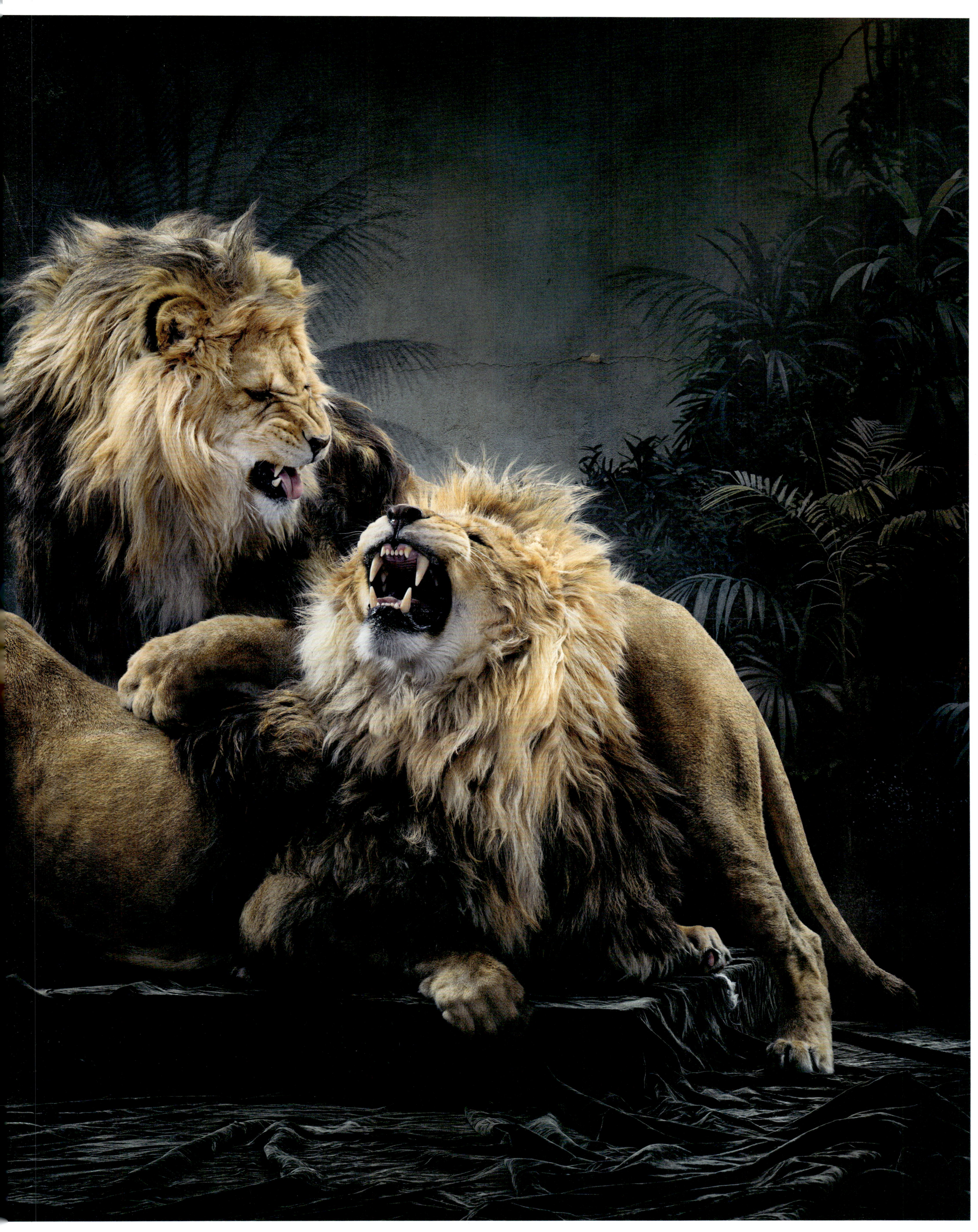

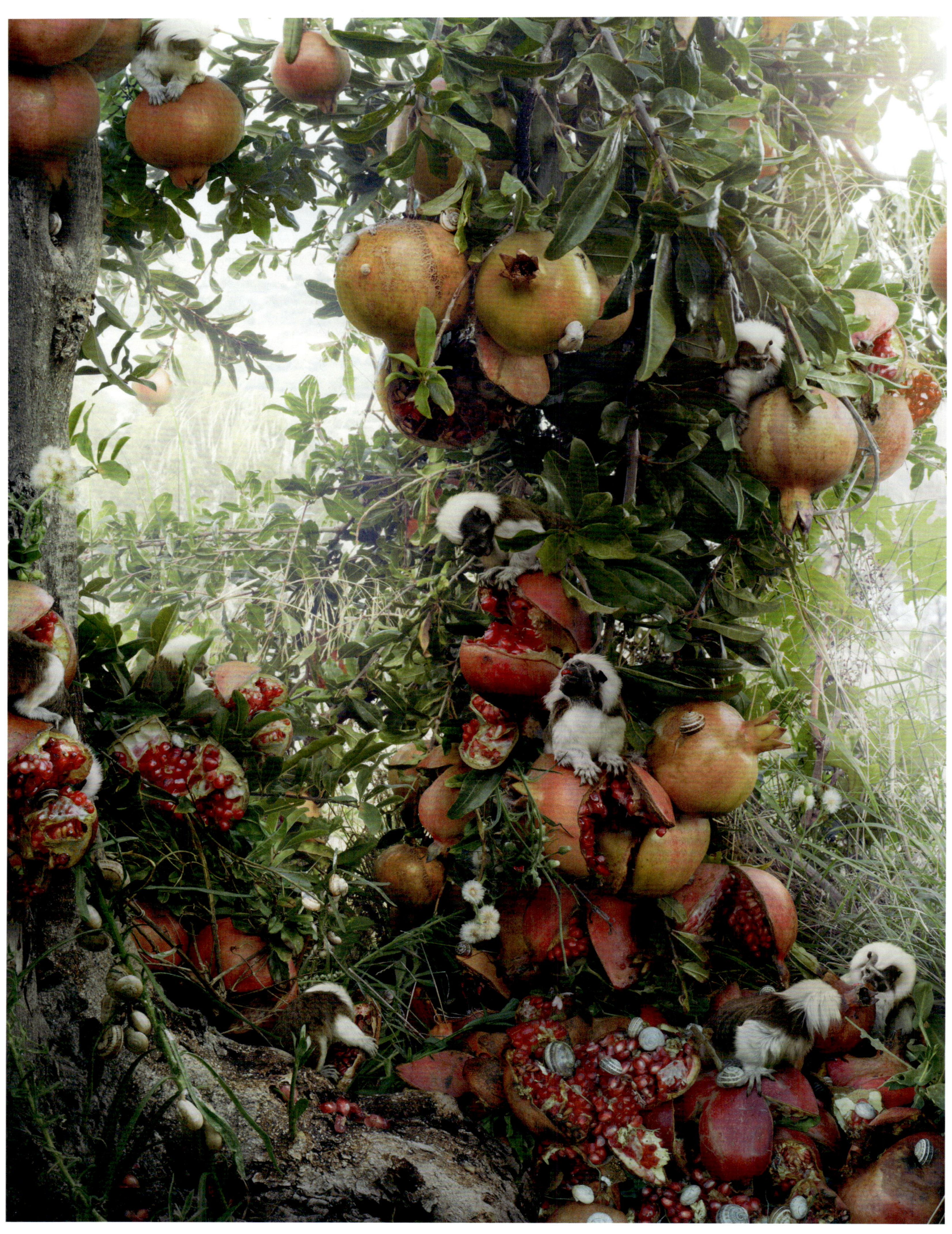

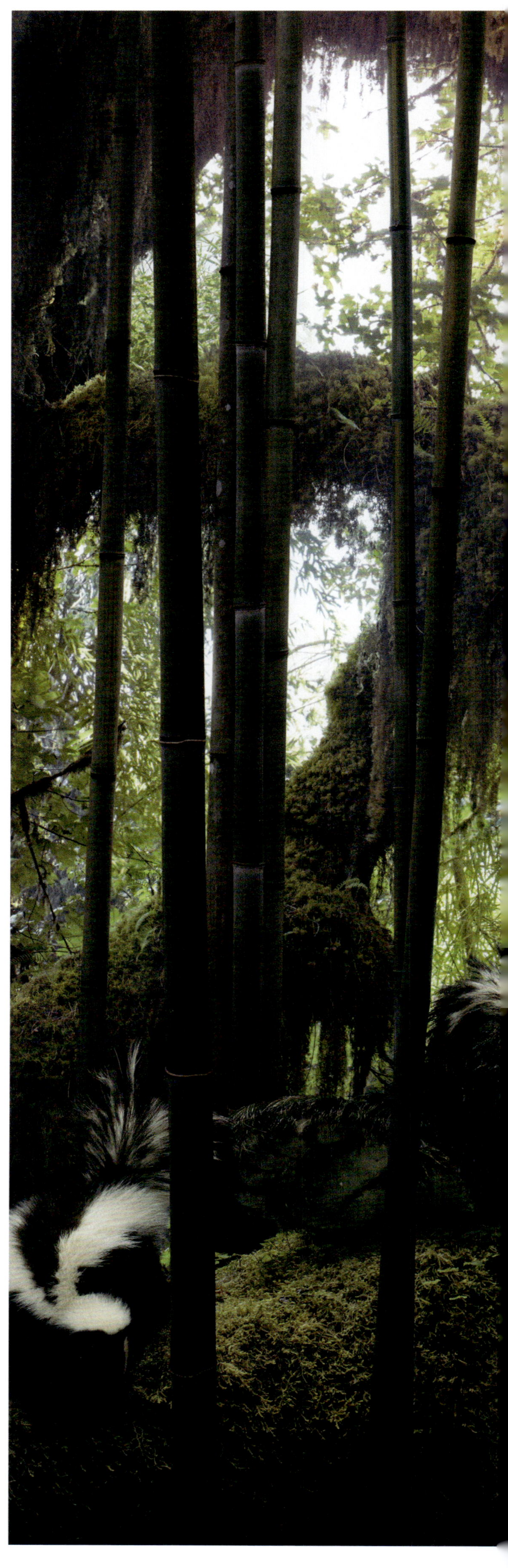

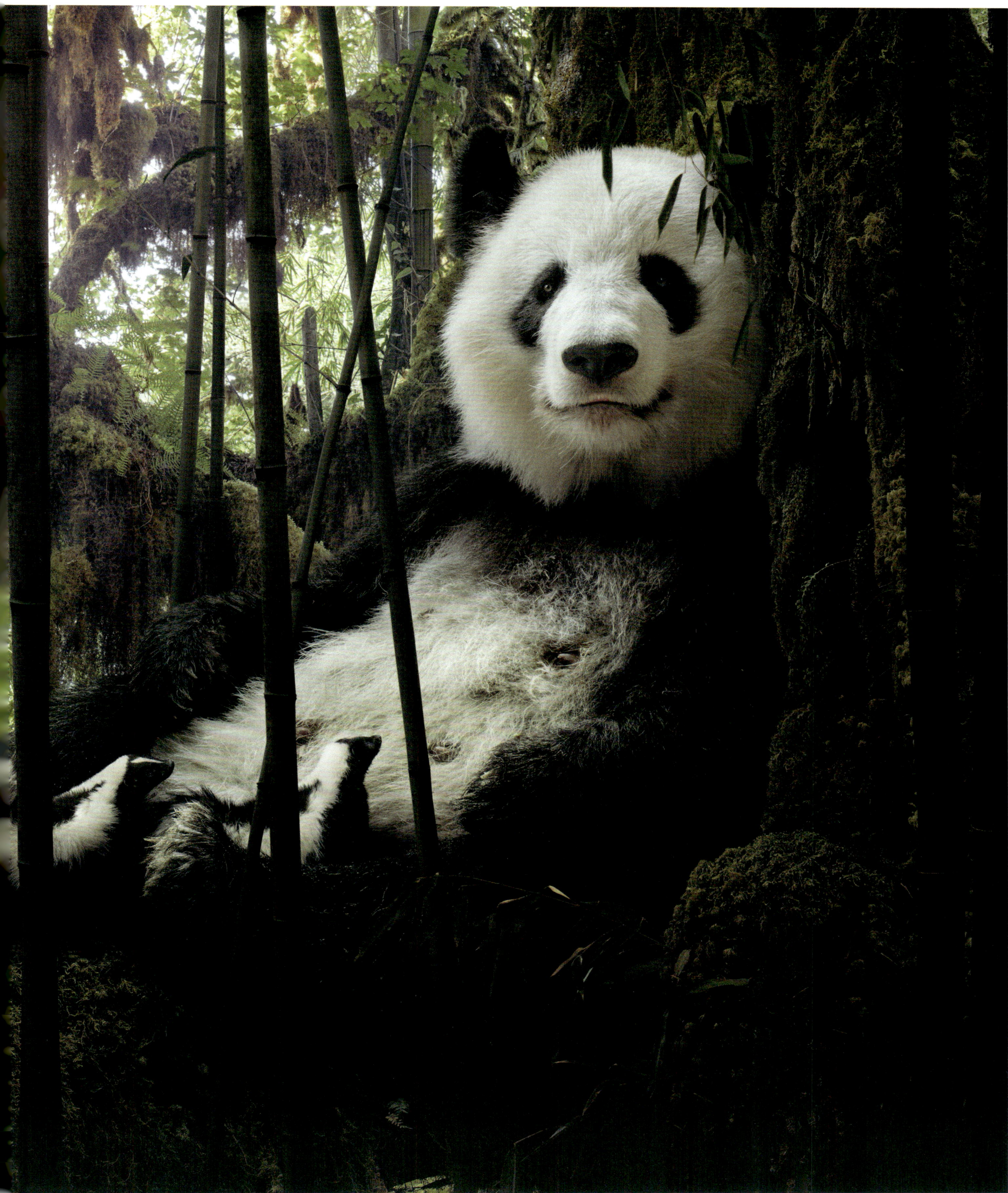

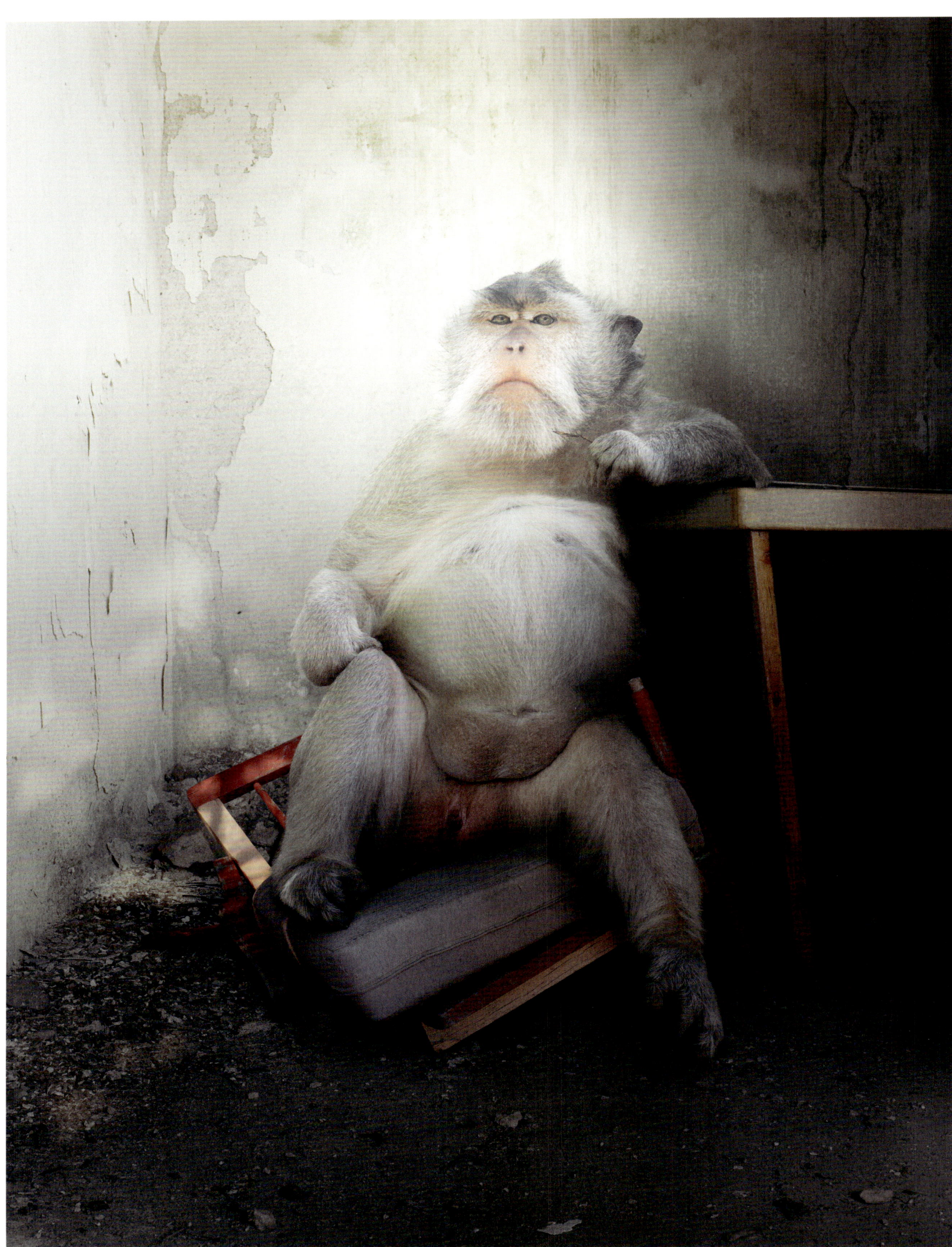

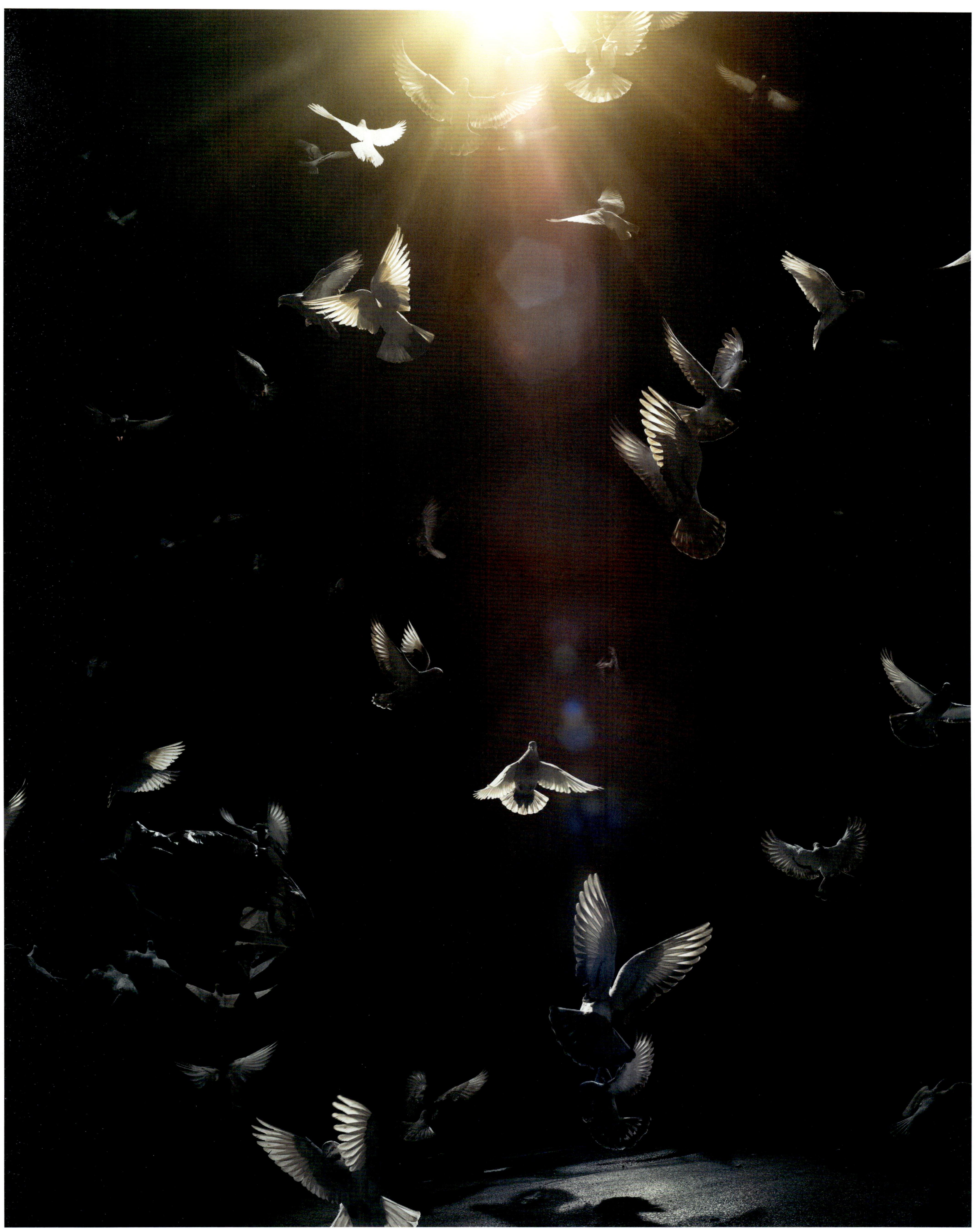

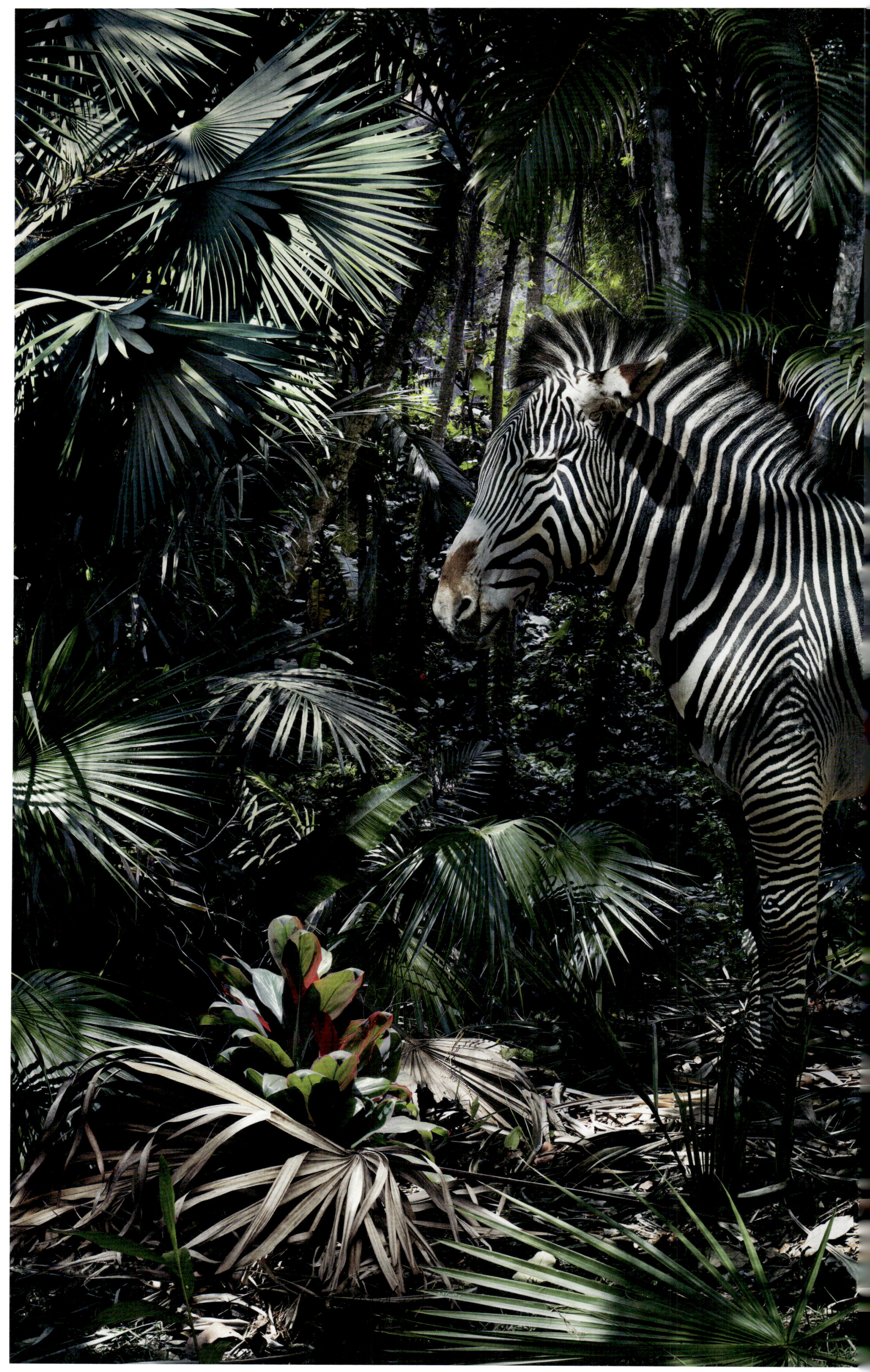

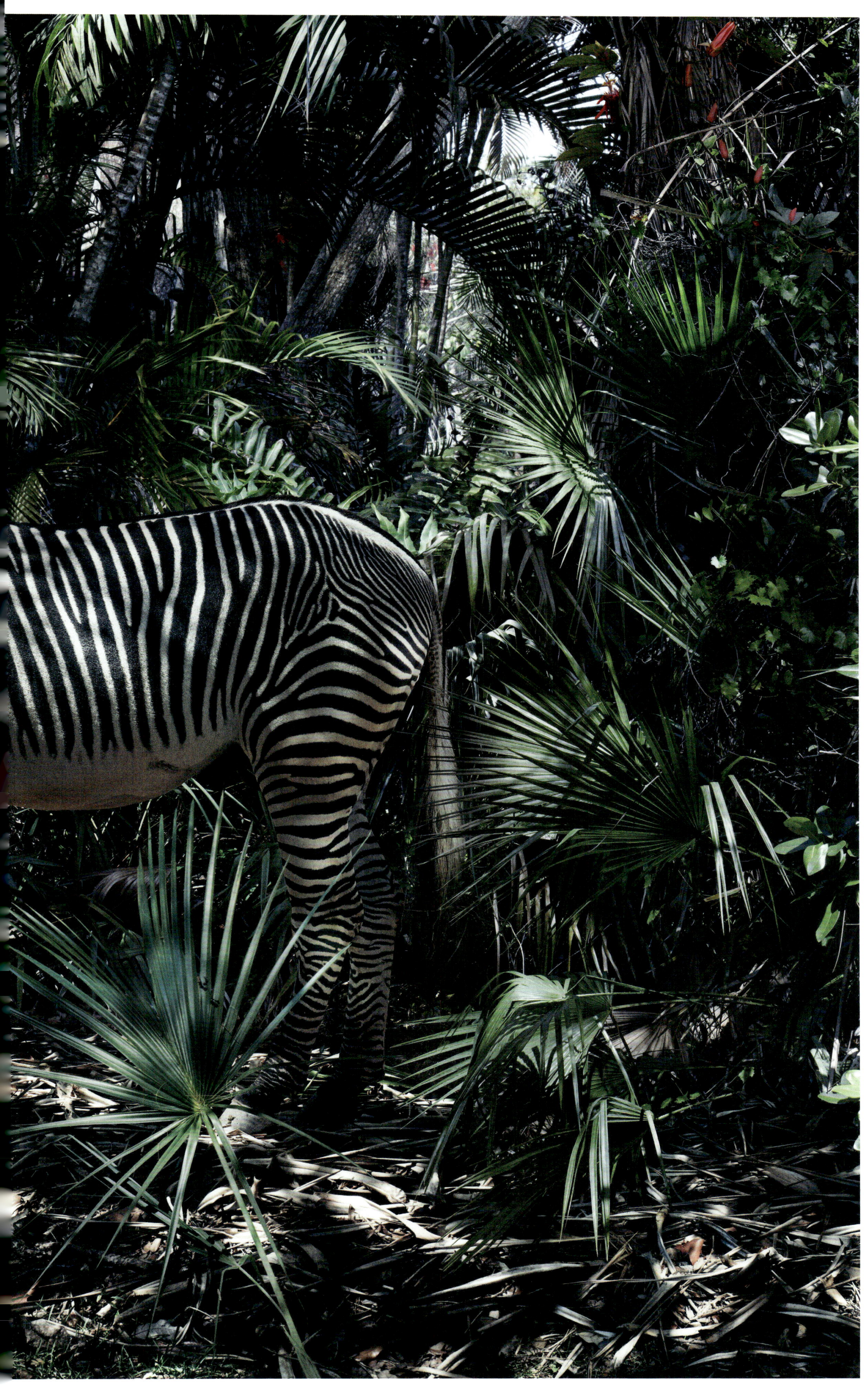

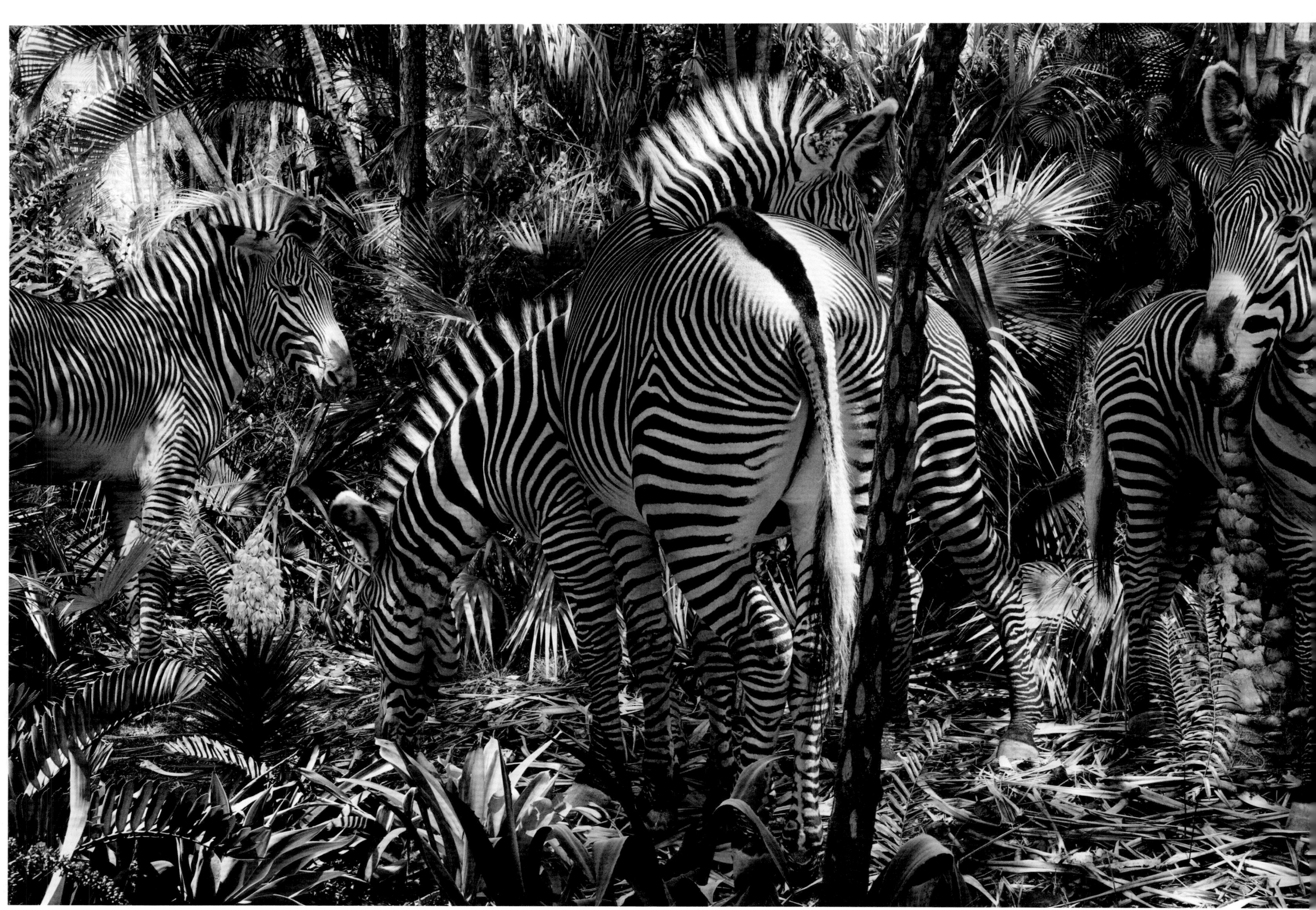

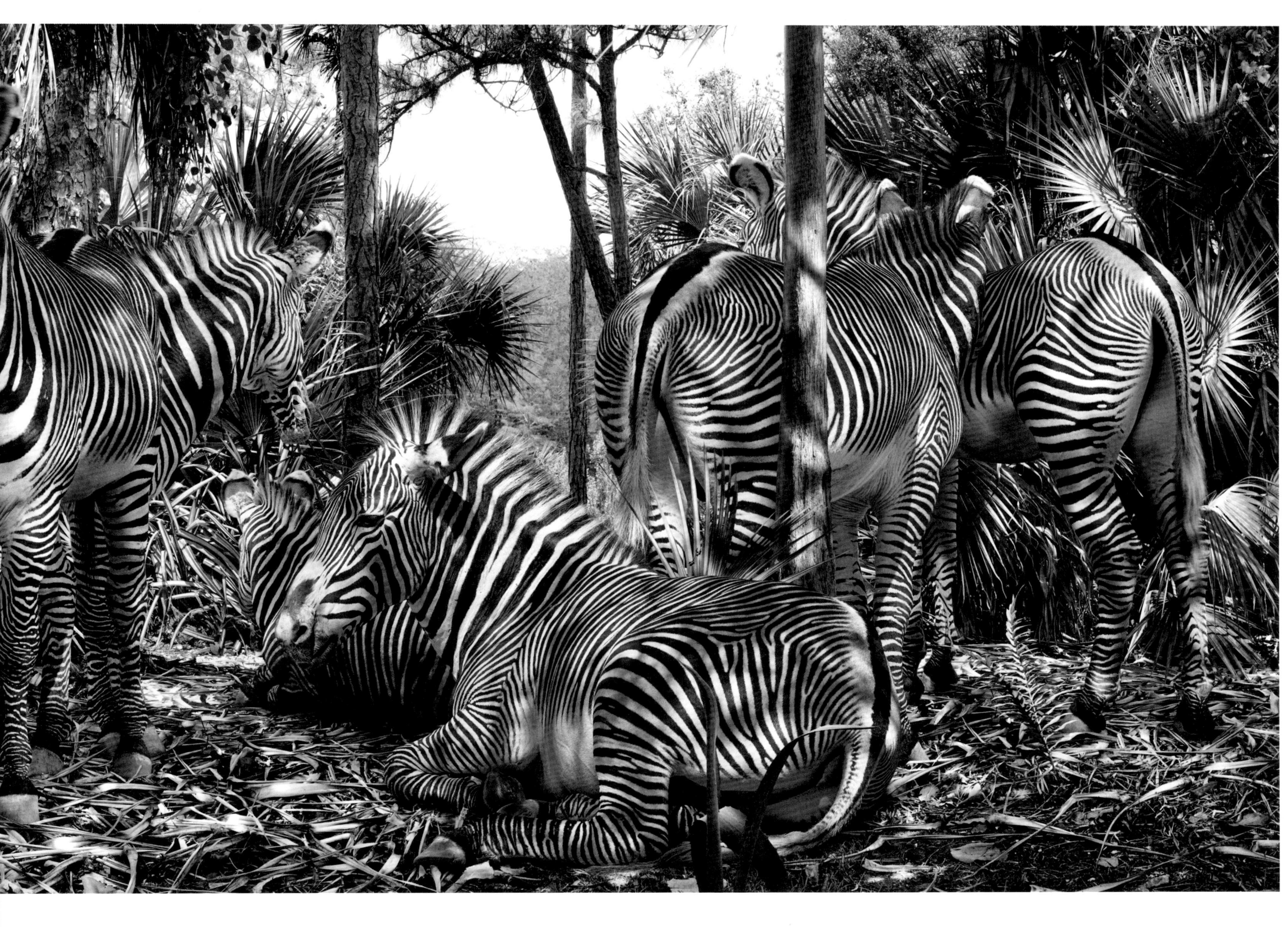

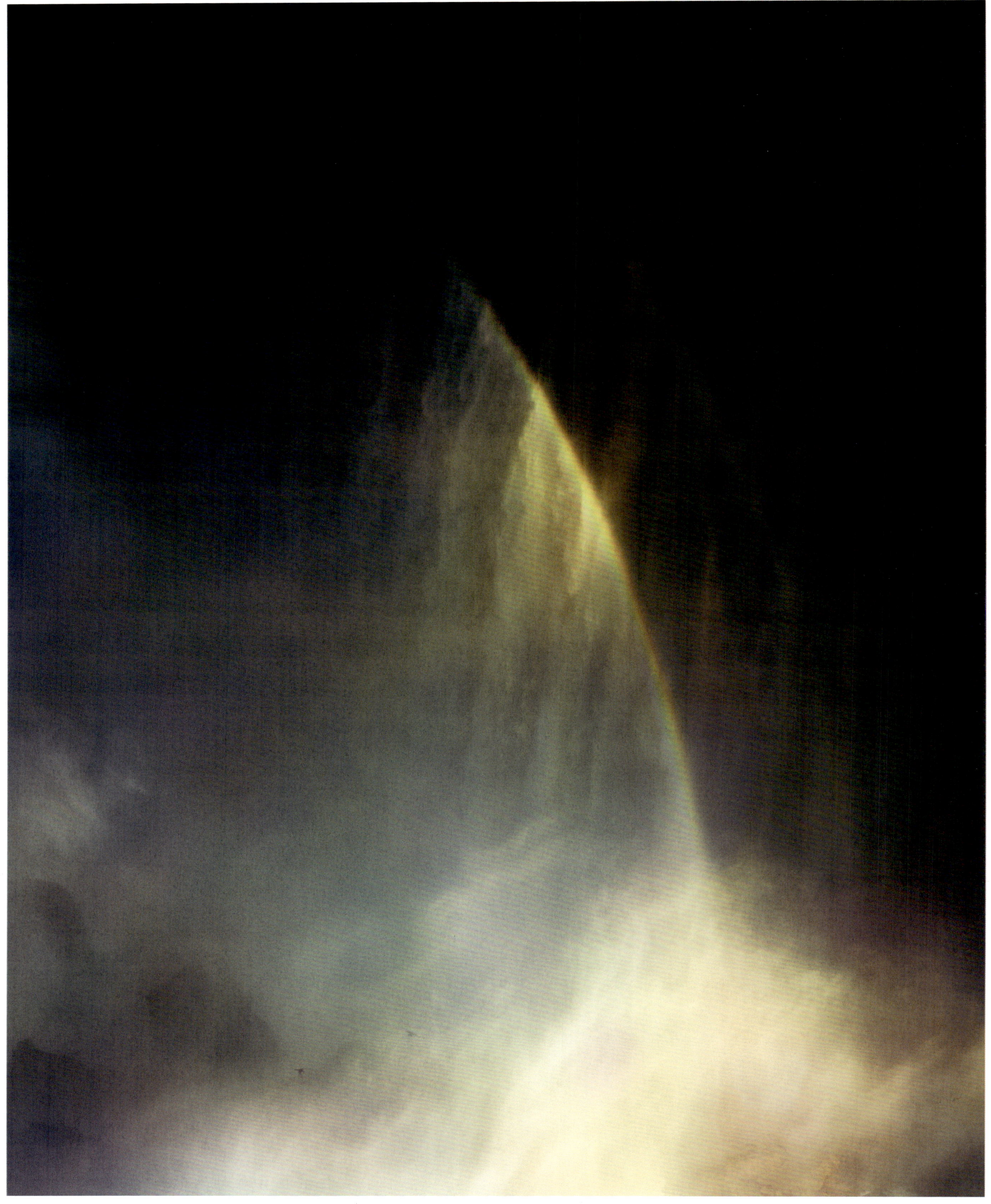

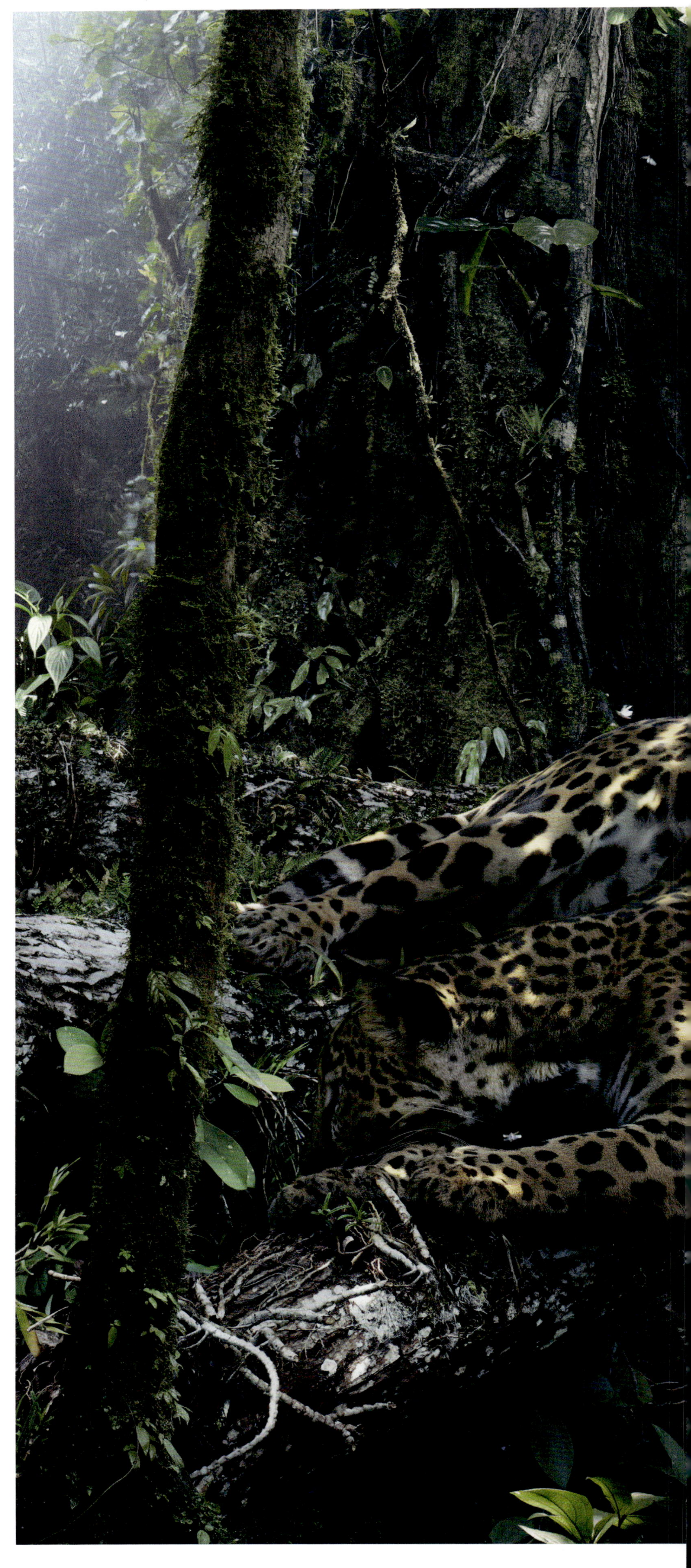

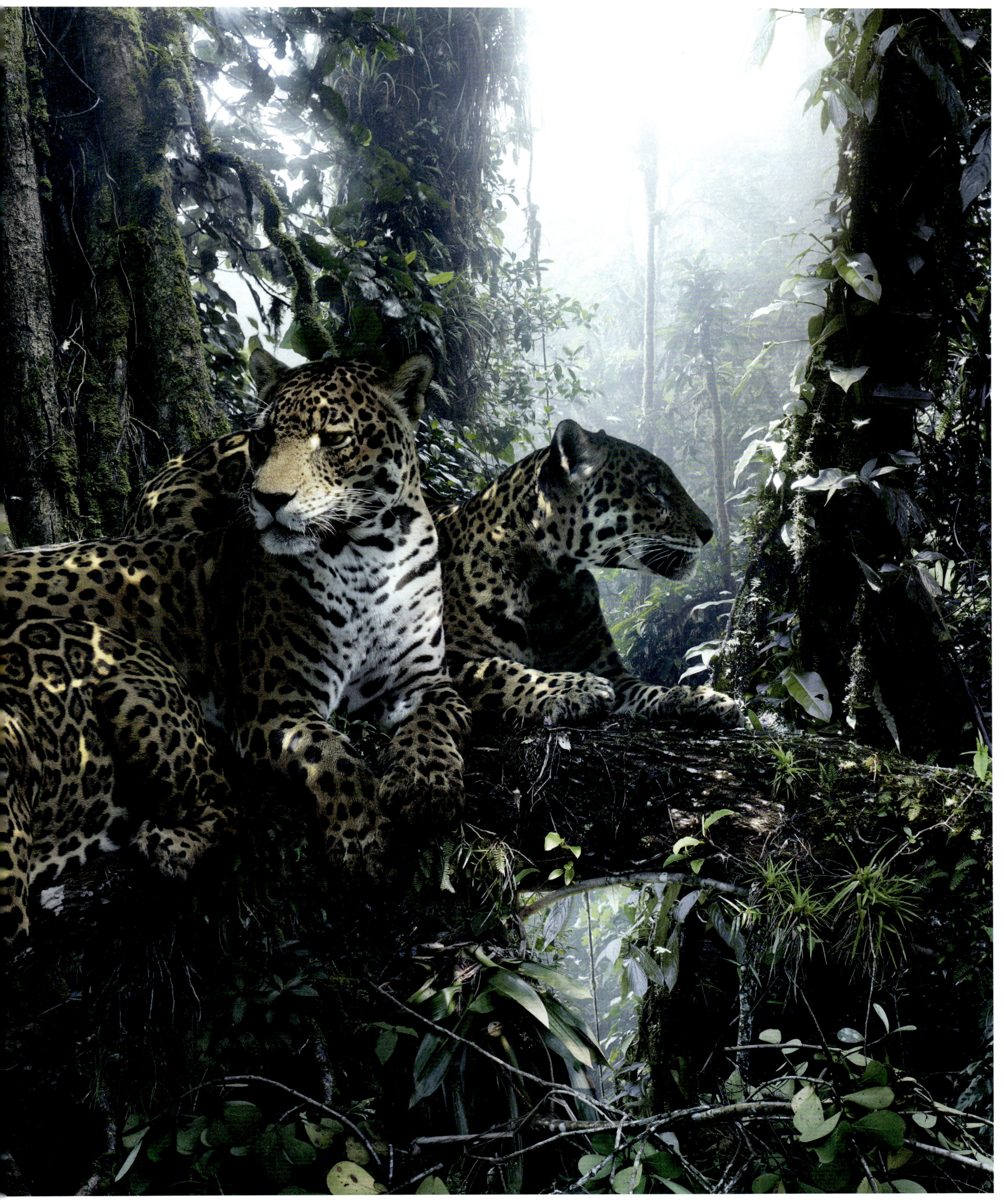

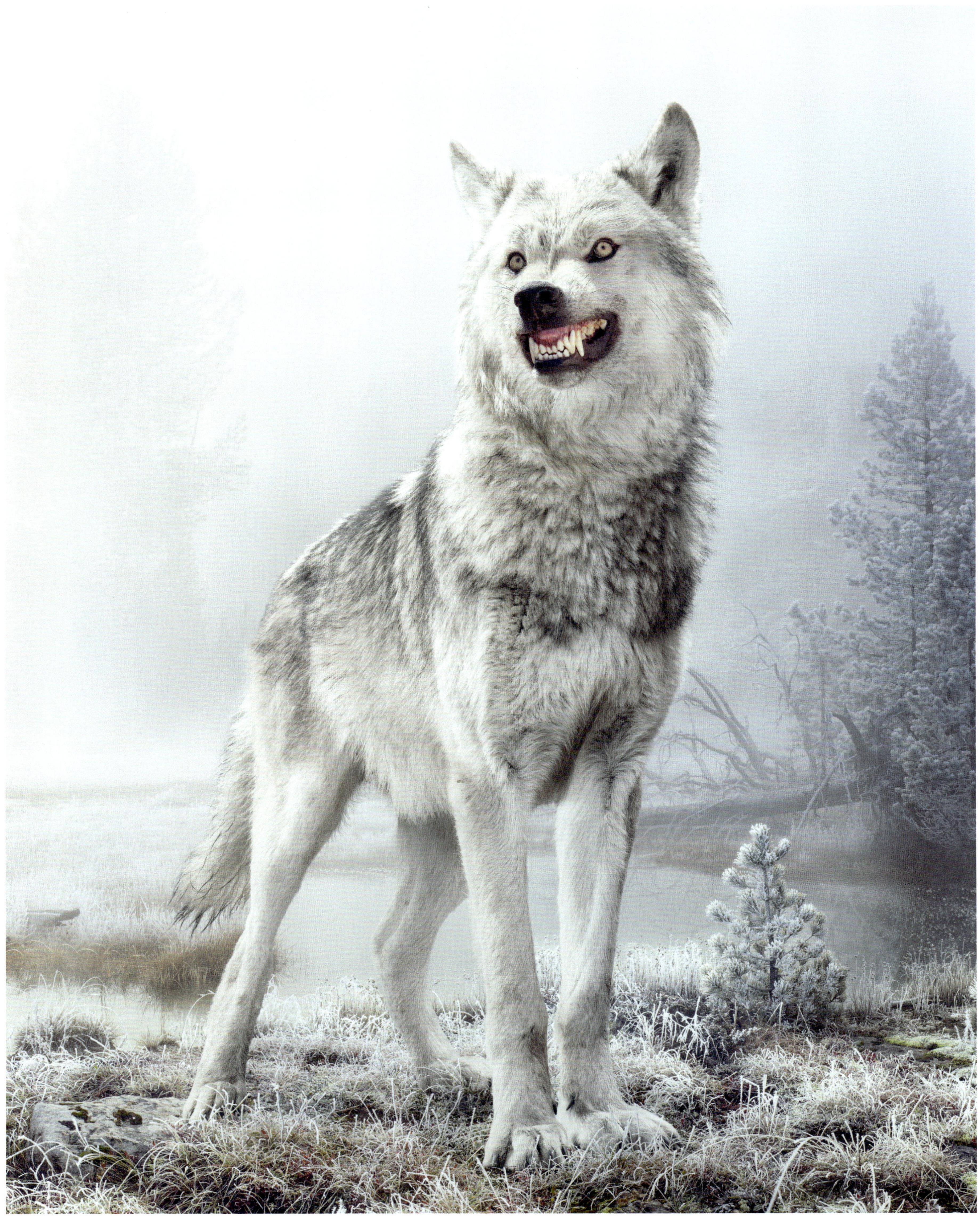

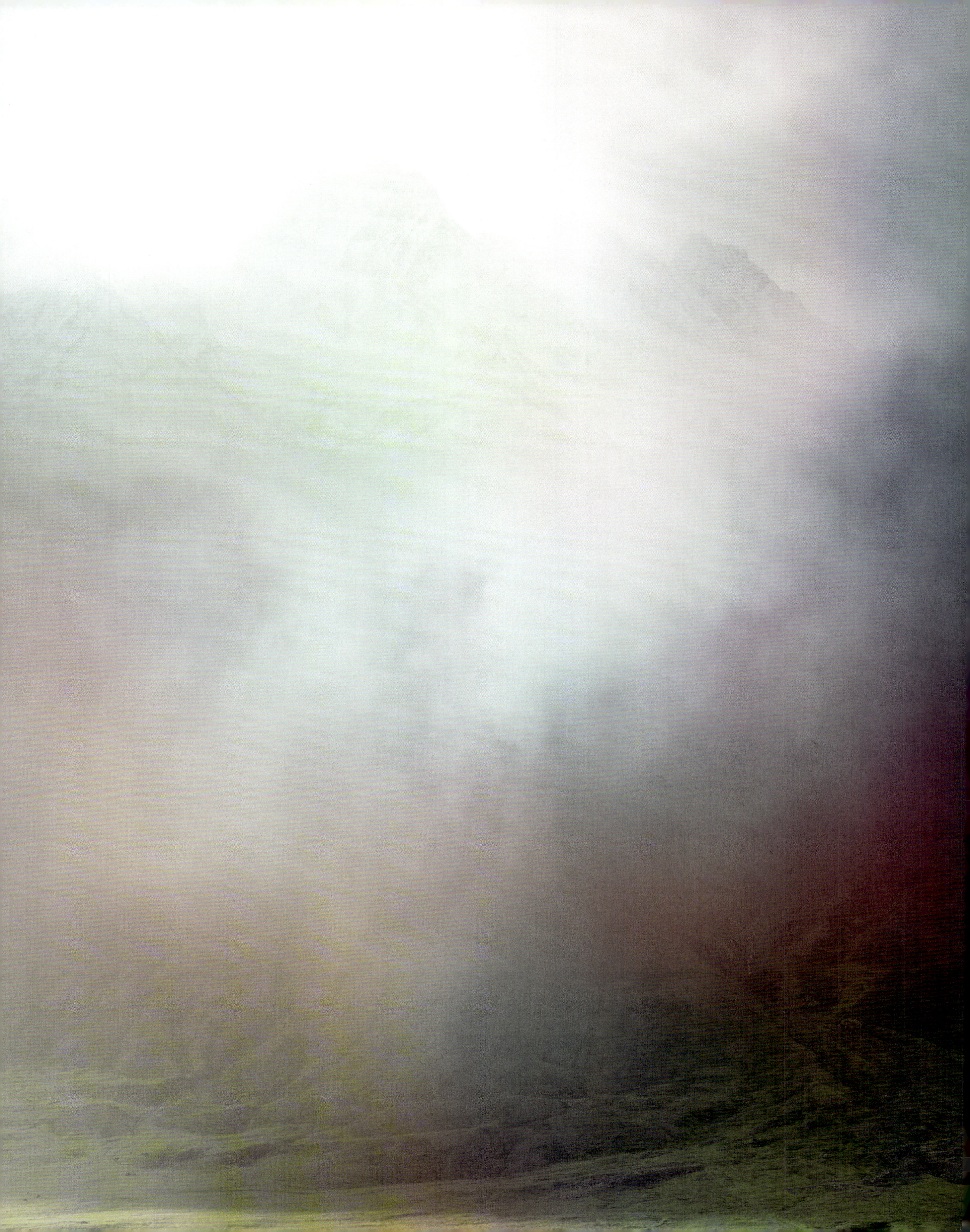

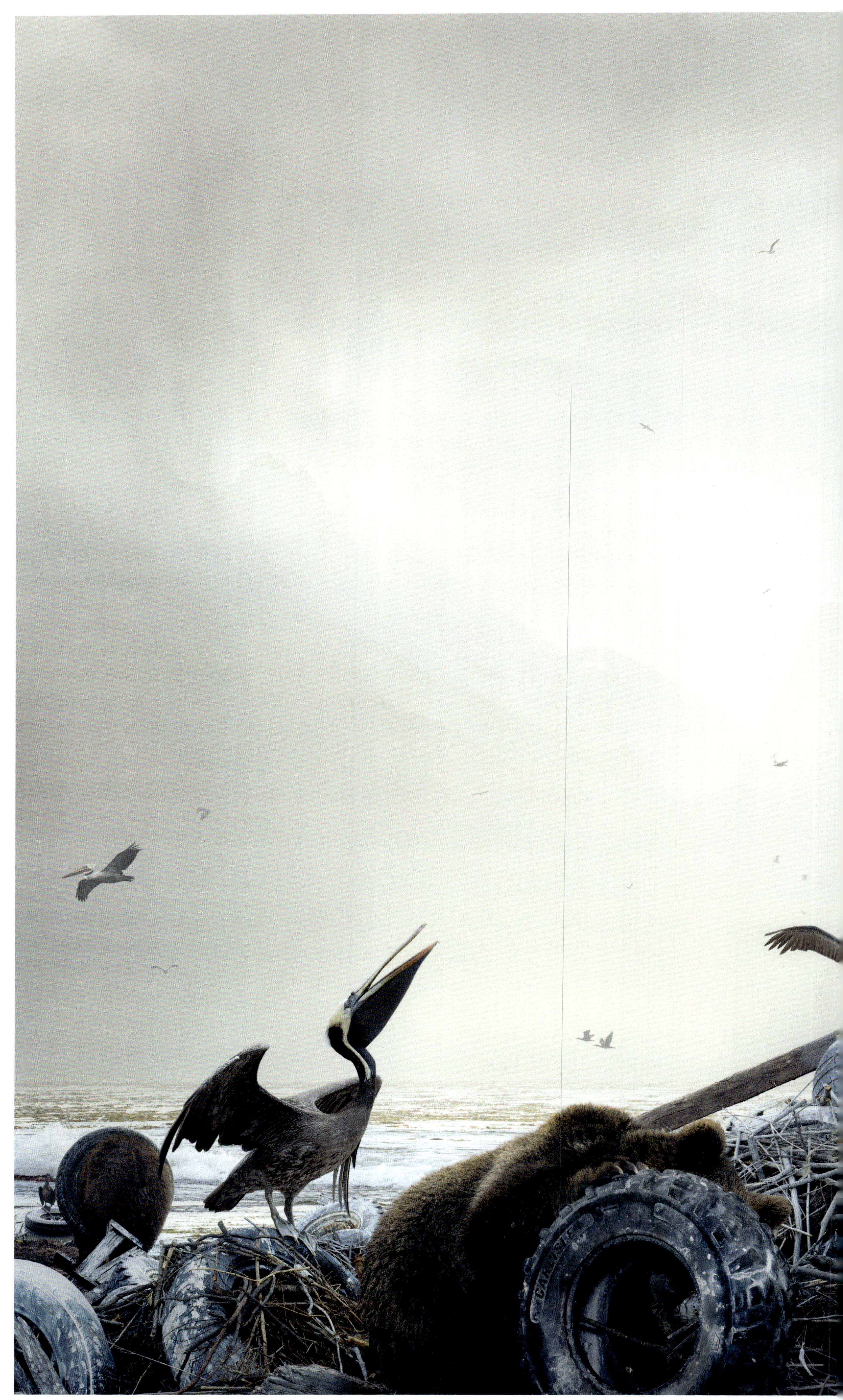

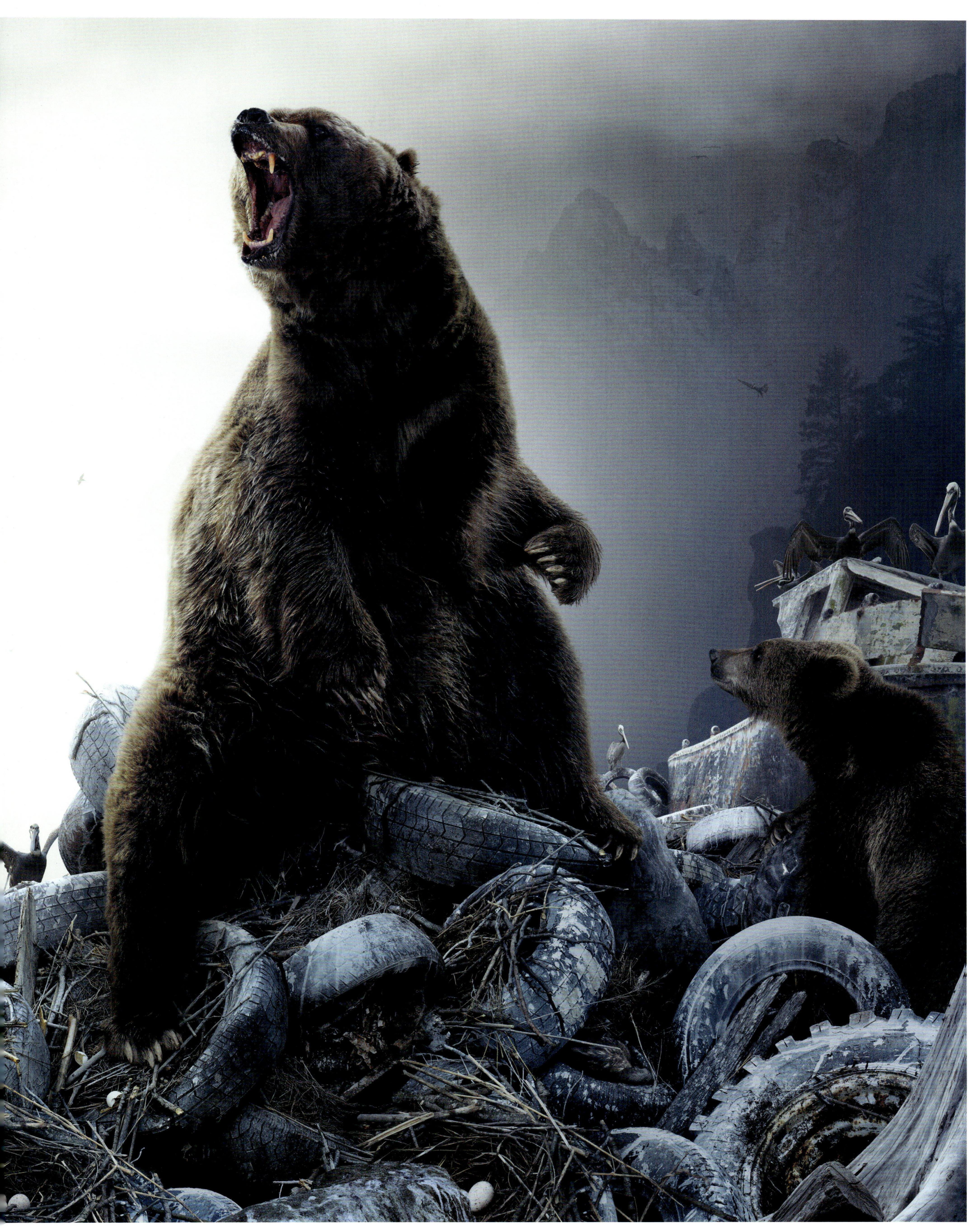

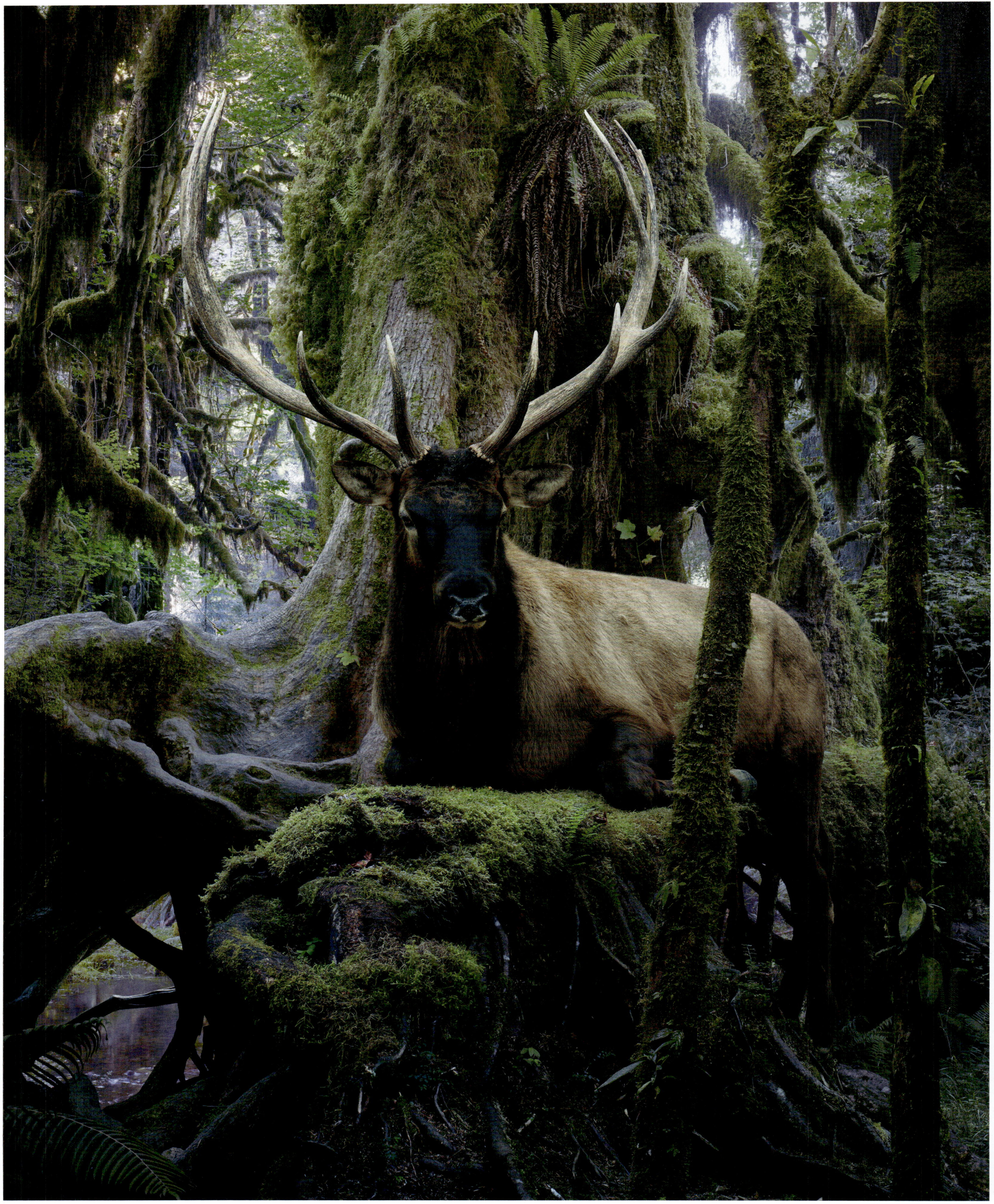

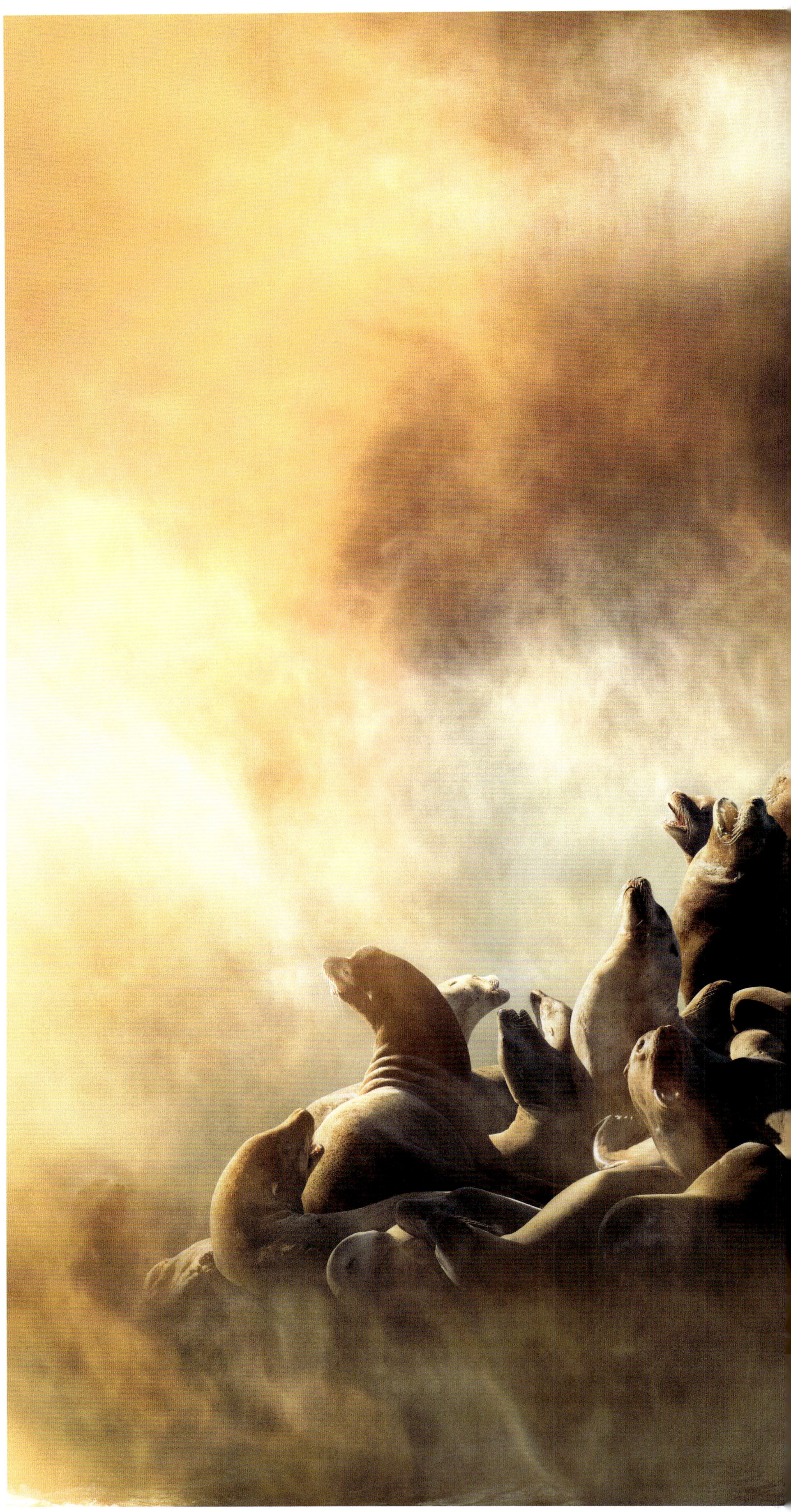

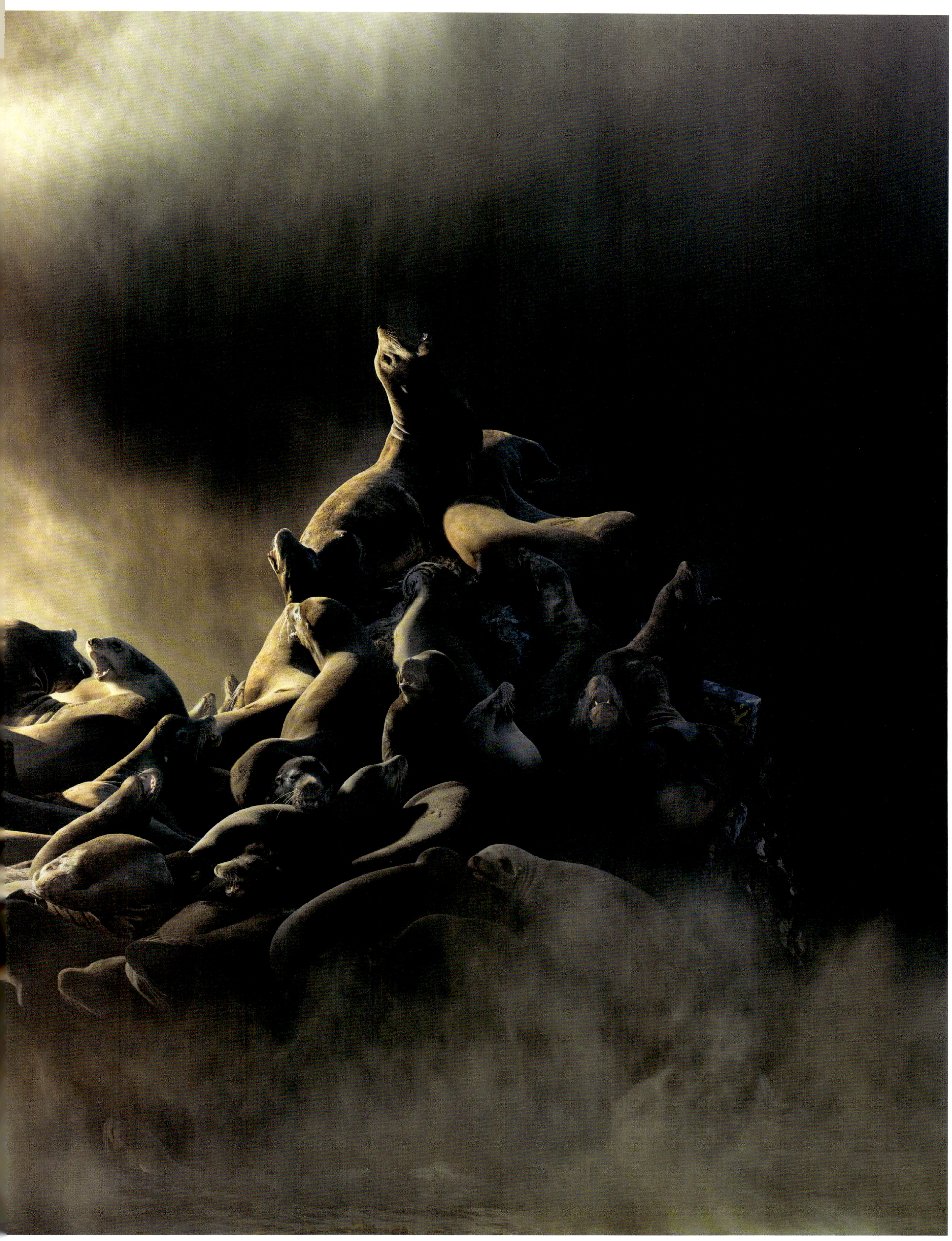

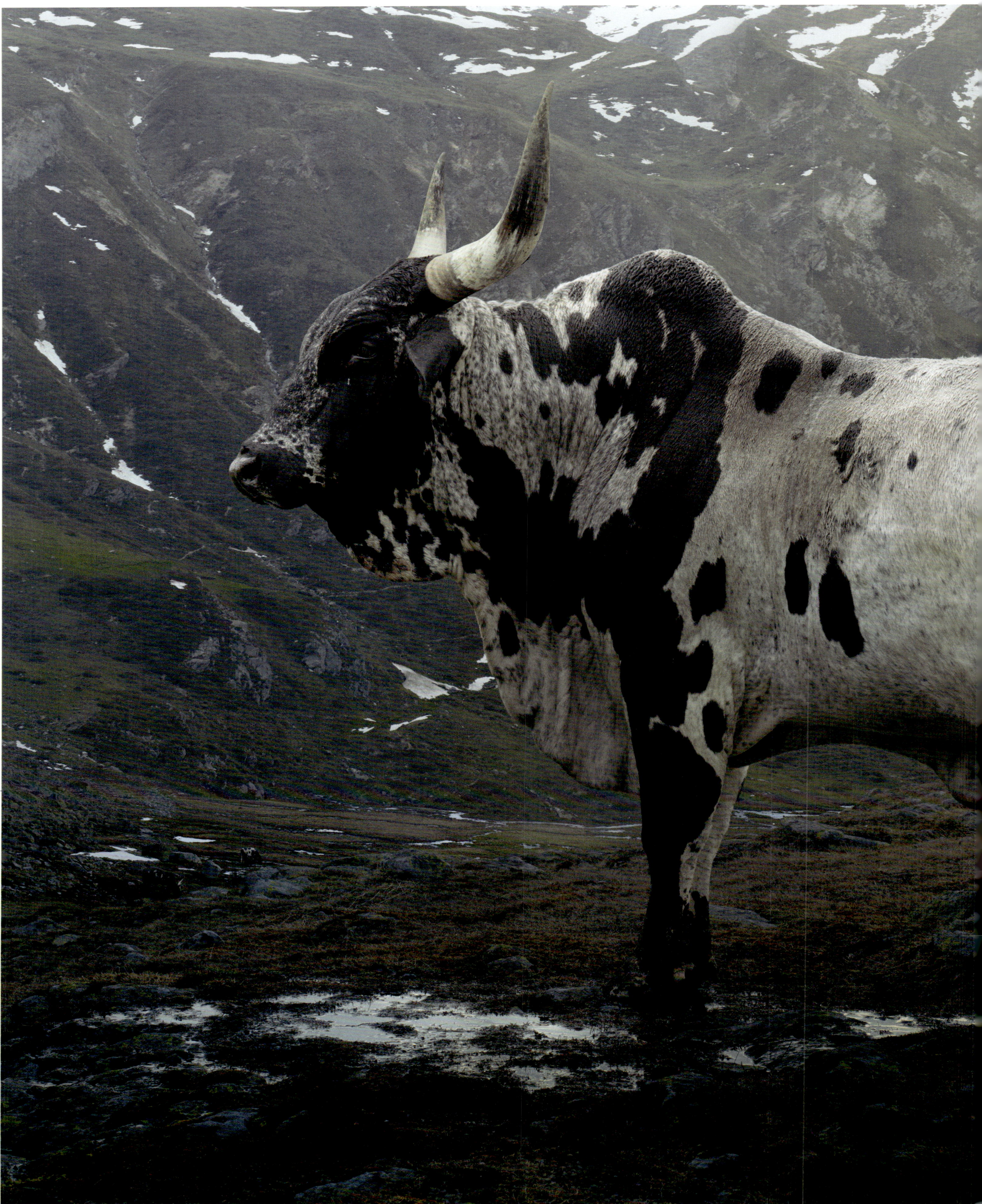

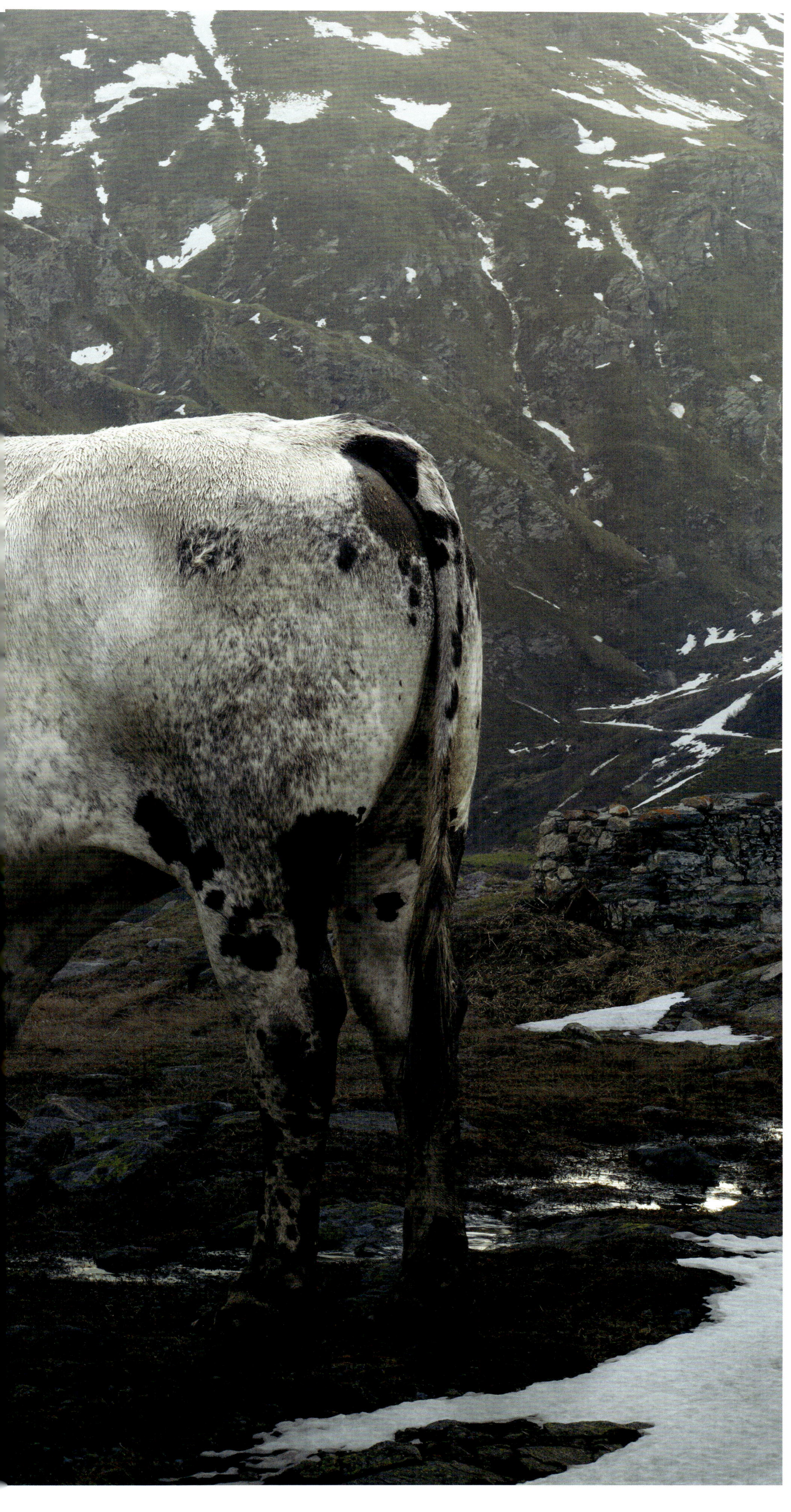

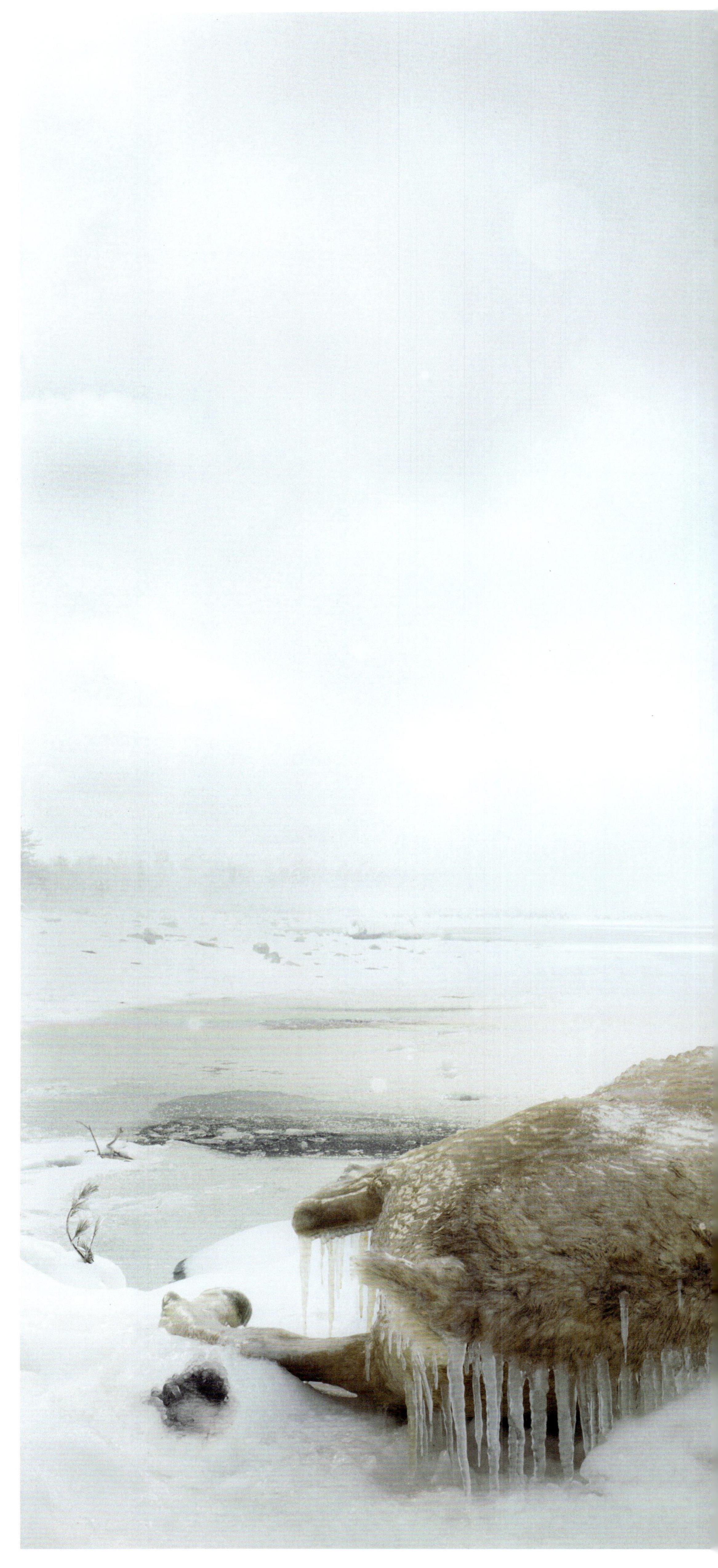

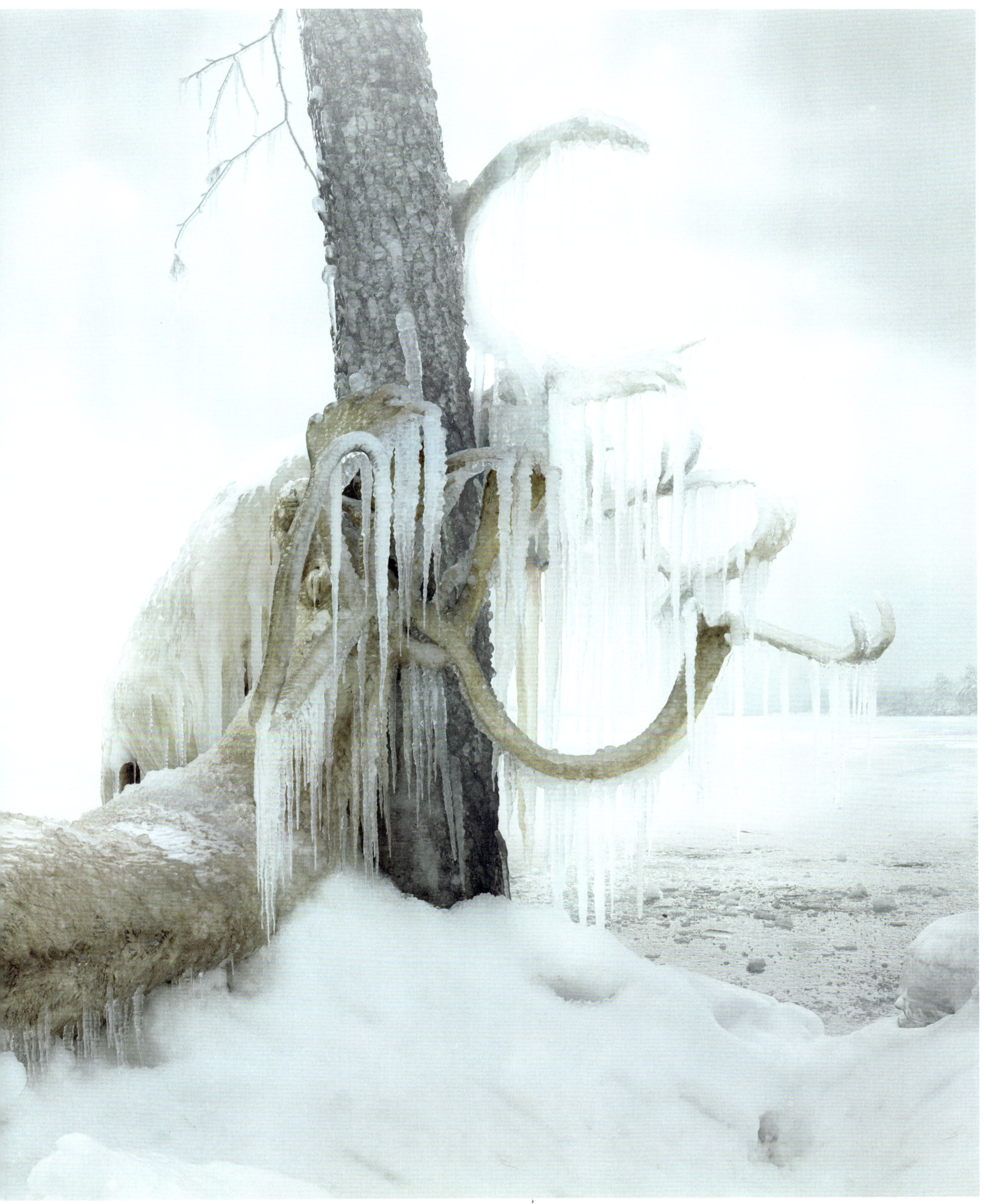

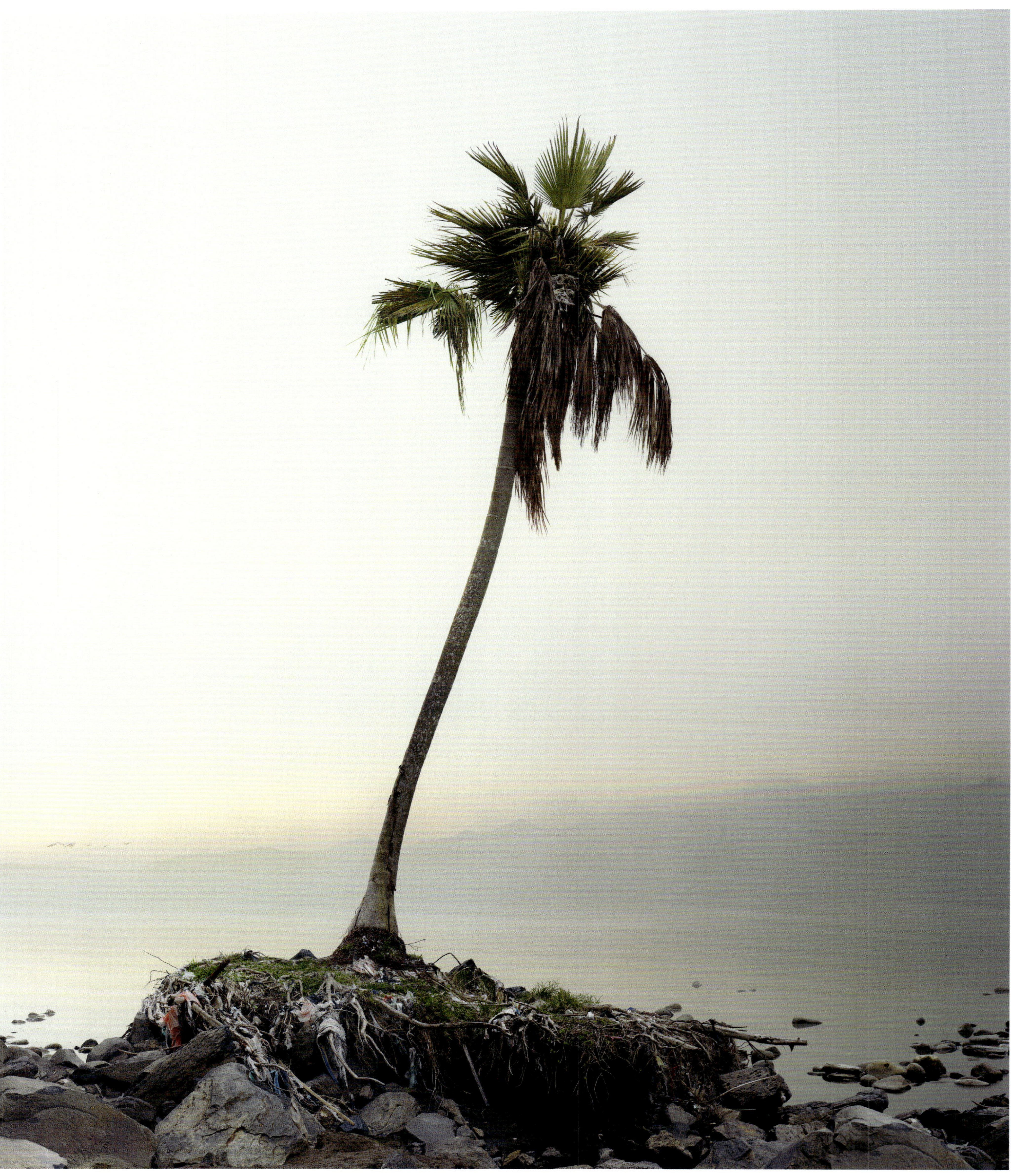

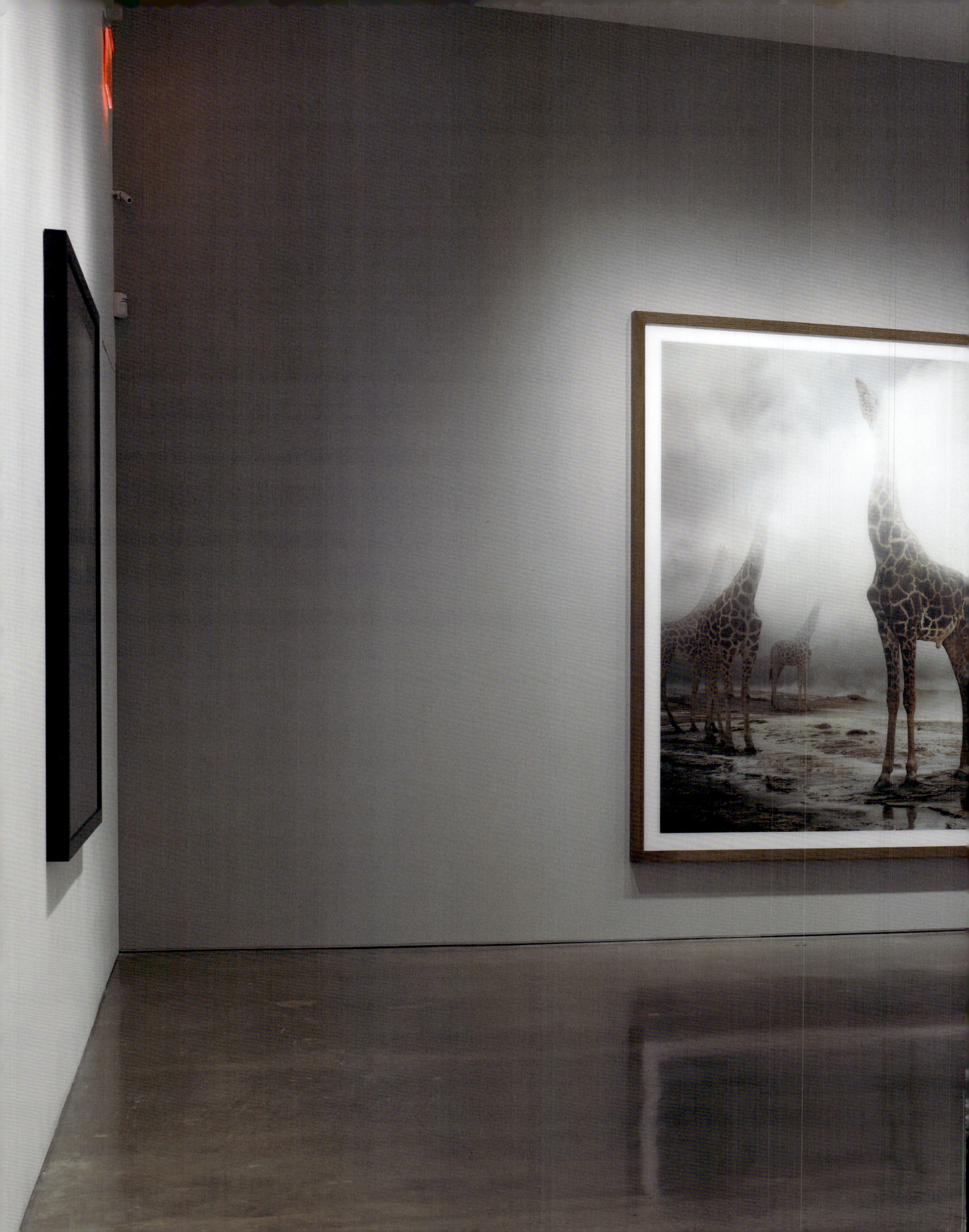

SIMEN JOHAN

Artwork © 2023 Simen Johan
Text © 2023 Hugo Fortin
All rights reserved.

The artist would like to acknowledge everyone who has exhibited, collected, published,
written about, awarded, assisted, appreciated, or otherwise supported his work,
with special thanks to Yossi Milo Gallery and powerHouse Books.

Published in the United States by powerHouse Books,
a division of powerHouse Cultural Entertainment, Inc.
32 Adams Street, Brooklyn, NY 11201-1021

www.powerHouseBooks.com

This first edition is limited to 3000 casebound copies.
Twenty-five copies are presented in a clamshell box with an
original print, signed and numbered by the artist for this edition.

Library of Congress Control Number: 2022946183
Regular edition: ISBN 978-1-64823-028-8
Limited edition: ISBN 978-1-64823-030-1

Printed in Italy

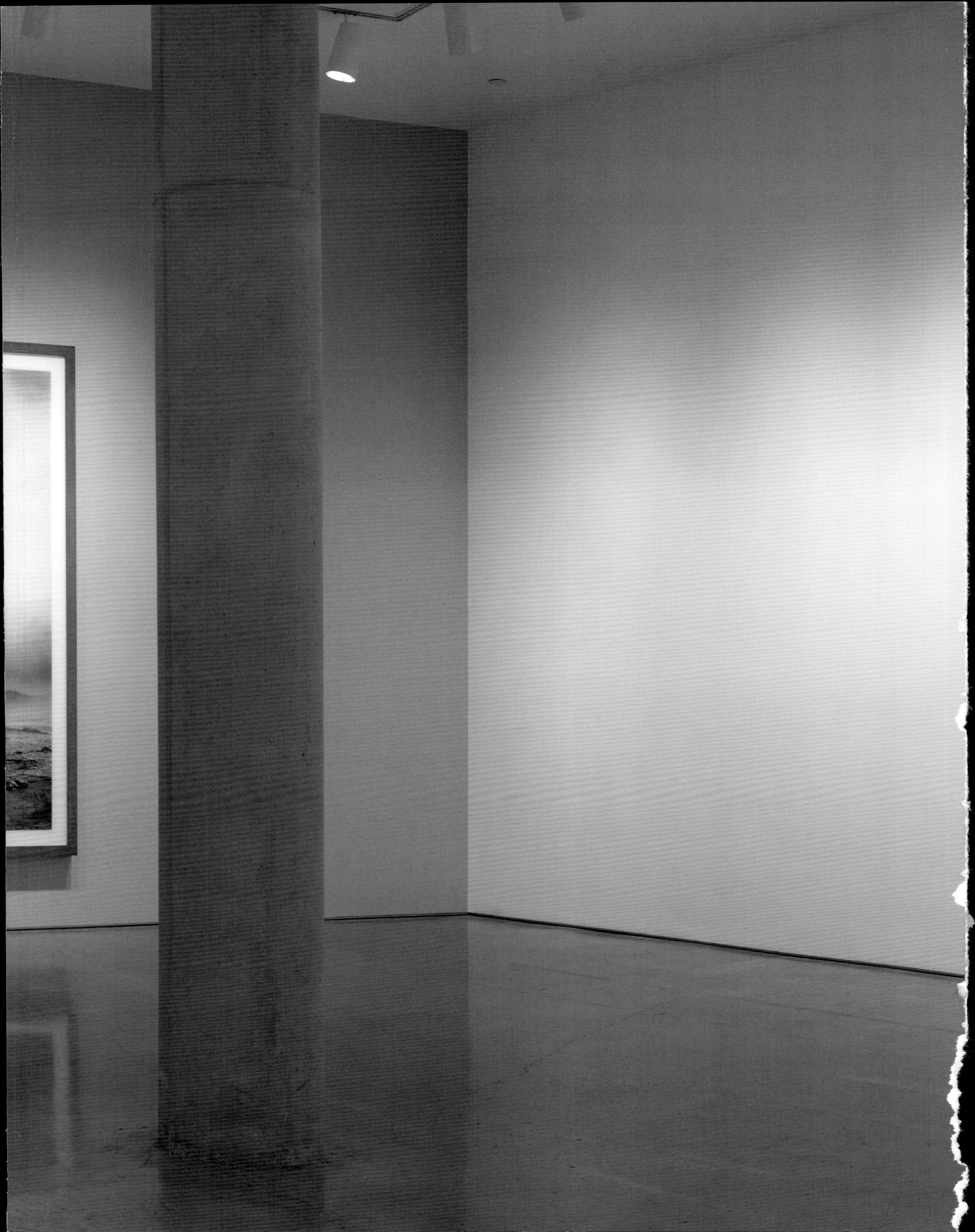

LIST OF WORKS

End paper
Gowanus Canal, 2013
Wallpaper, dimensions variable

Page 5
Untitled #164, 2011
64 x 81 in. (162.6 x 205.7 cm)

Page 6
Untitled #166, 2012
41.5 x 53.5 in. (105.4 x 135.9 cm)

Page 9
Untitled #172, 2013
73 x 87.5 in. (185.4 x 222.3 cm)

Page 10
Untitled #163, 2011
42 x 51 in. (106.7 x 129.5 cm)

Page 13
Untitled #155, 2010
29 x 35 in. (73 .7 x 88.9 cm)

Page 14–15
Untitled #153, 2008
96.5 x 64 in. (245.1 x 162.6 cm)

Page 16
Untitled #138, 2006
64 x 74 in. (162.6 x 188 cm)

Page 19
Untitled #132, 2005
53 x 53 in. (134.6 x 134.6 cm)

Page 20
Untitled #177, 2013
64 x 78.5 in. (162.6 x 199.4 cm)

Page 22–23
Untitled #140, 2007
63.6 x 53 in. (161.5 x 134.6 cm)

Page 24
Untitled #137, 2006
40 x 48 in. (101.6 x 121.9 cm)

Page 26–27
Untitled #133, 2006
85.5 x 64 in. (217.2 x 162.6 cm)

Page 28
Untitled #162, 2010
25 x 32 in. (63.5 x 81.3 cm)

Page 30–31
Untitled #171, 2012
77.5 x 60 in. (196.9 x 152.4 cm)

Page 32–33
Untitled #174, 2013
70 x 58 in. (177.8 x 147.3 cm)

Page 35
Untitled #178, 2013
42.5 x 56 in. (108 x 142.2 cm)

Page 36–37
Untitled #168, 2011
89.5 x 64 in. (227.3 x 162.6 cm)

Page 38–39
Untitled #201, 2019
105.25 x 55 in. (267.3 x 139.7 cm)

Page 40–41
Untitled #198, 2019
37.5 x 30 in. (95.3 x 76.2 cm)

Page 42
Untitled #193, 2018
26.5 x 35.25 in. (67.3 x 89.5 cm)

Page 44–45
Untitled #196, 2018
77 x 69 in. (195.6 x 175.3 cm)

Page 46
Untitled #176, 2013
26 x 33.25 in. (66 x 84.5 cm)

Page 48–49
Untitled #203, 2019
68.5 x 57.25 in. (174 x 145.4 cm)

Page 50
Untitled #199, 2019
34.5 x 44.5 in. (87.6 x 113 cm)

Page 53
Untitled #187, 2016
64 x 80 in. (162.6 x 203.2 cm)

Page 54–55
Untitled #181, 2015
79.5 x 62 in. (201.9 x 157.5 cm)

Page 56–57
Untitled #182, 2016
162 x 54 in. (411.5 x 137.2 cm)

Page 58
Untitled #186, 2016
46 x 56 in. (116.8 x 142.2 cm)

Page 60–61
Untitled #183, 2015
71.5 x 55 in. (181.6 x 139.7 cm)

Page 62
Untitled #185, 2016
44 x 55 in. (111.8 x 139.7 cm)

Page 65
Untitled #195, 2018
40 x 49.5 in. (101.6 x 125.7 cm)

Page 66
Untitled #179, 2013
80 x 95.5 in. (203.2 x 242.6 cm)

Page 68–69
Untitled #200, 2019
119.25 x 83.5 in. (302.9 x 212.1 cm)

Page 70
Untitled #194, 2018
64 x 77.25 in. (162.6 x 196.2 cm)

Page 72–73
Untitled #188, 2015
94.25 x 71 in. (239.4 x 180.3 cm)

Page 74–75
Untitled #202, 2019
89 x 64.75 in. (226.1 x 164.5 cm)

Page 76–77
Untitled #159, 2010
73 x 56 in. (185.4 x 142.2 cm)

Page 78
Untitled #167, 2011
64 x 73 in. (162.6 x 185.4 cm)

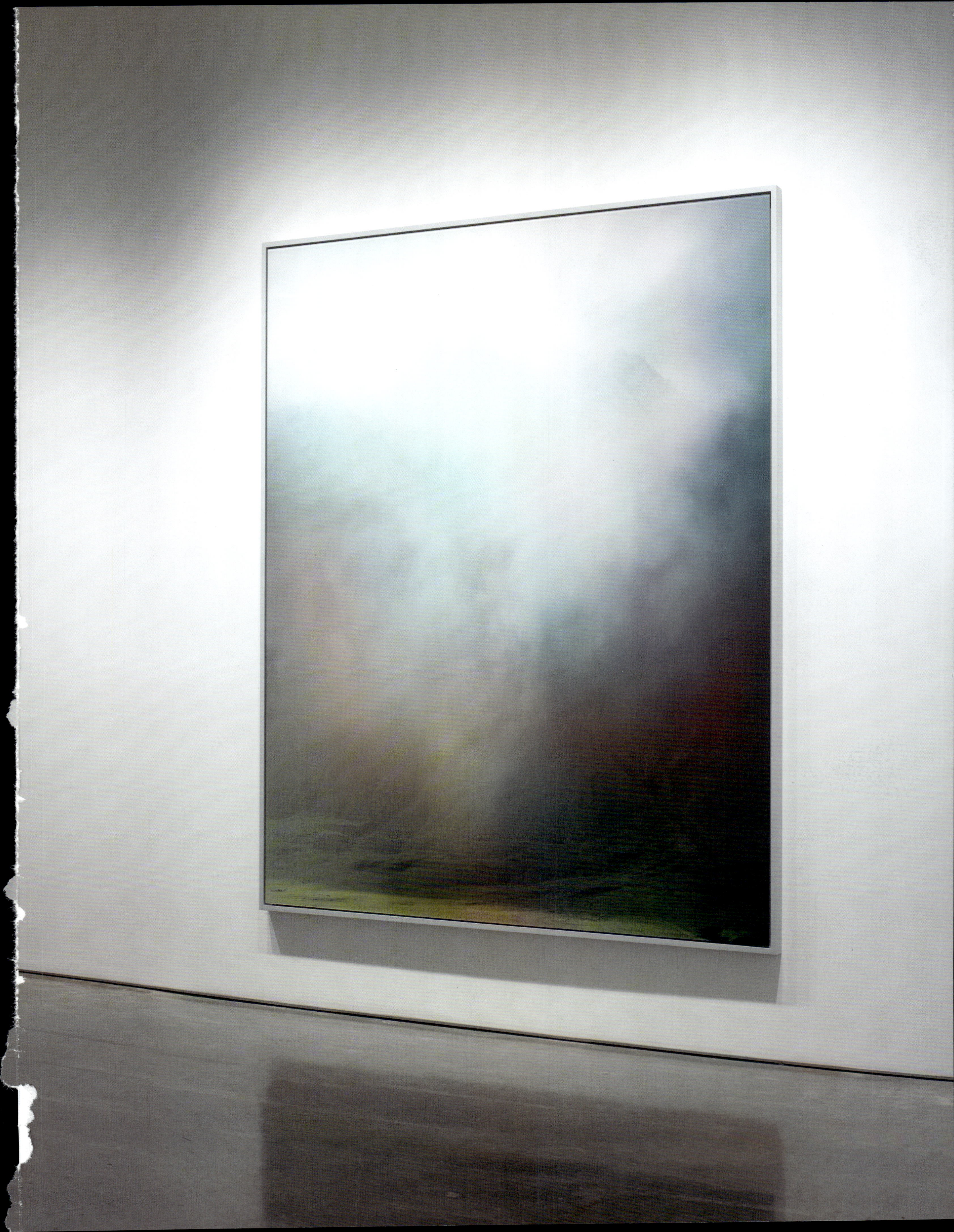

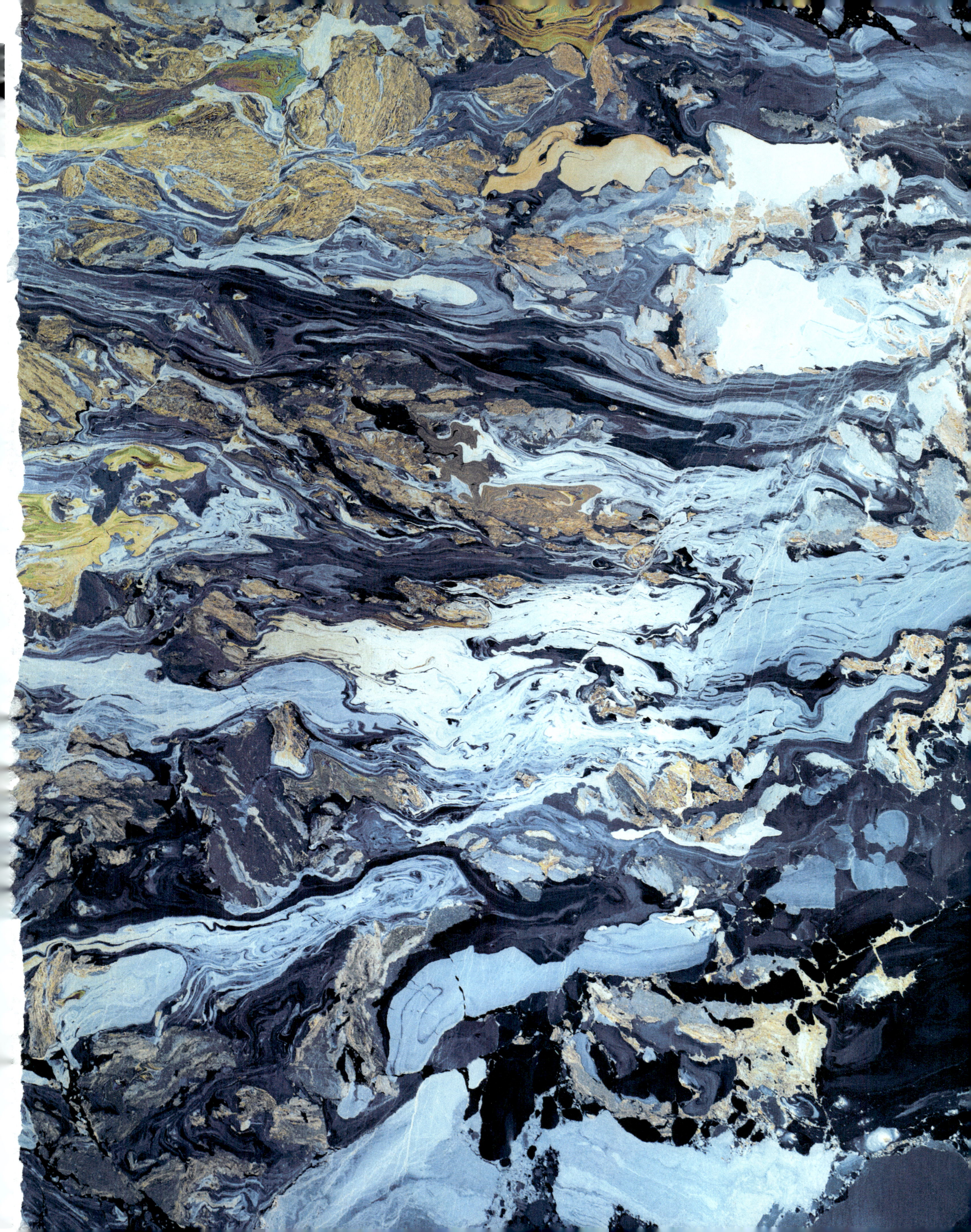

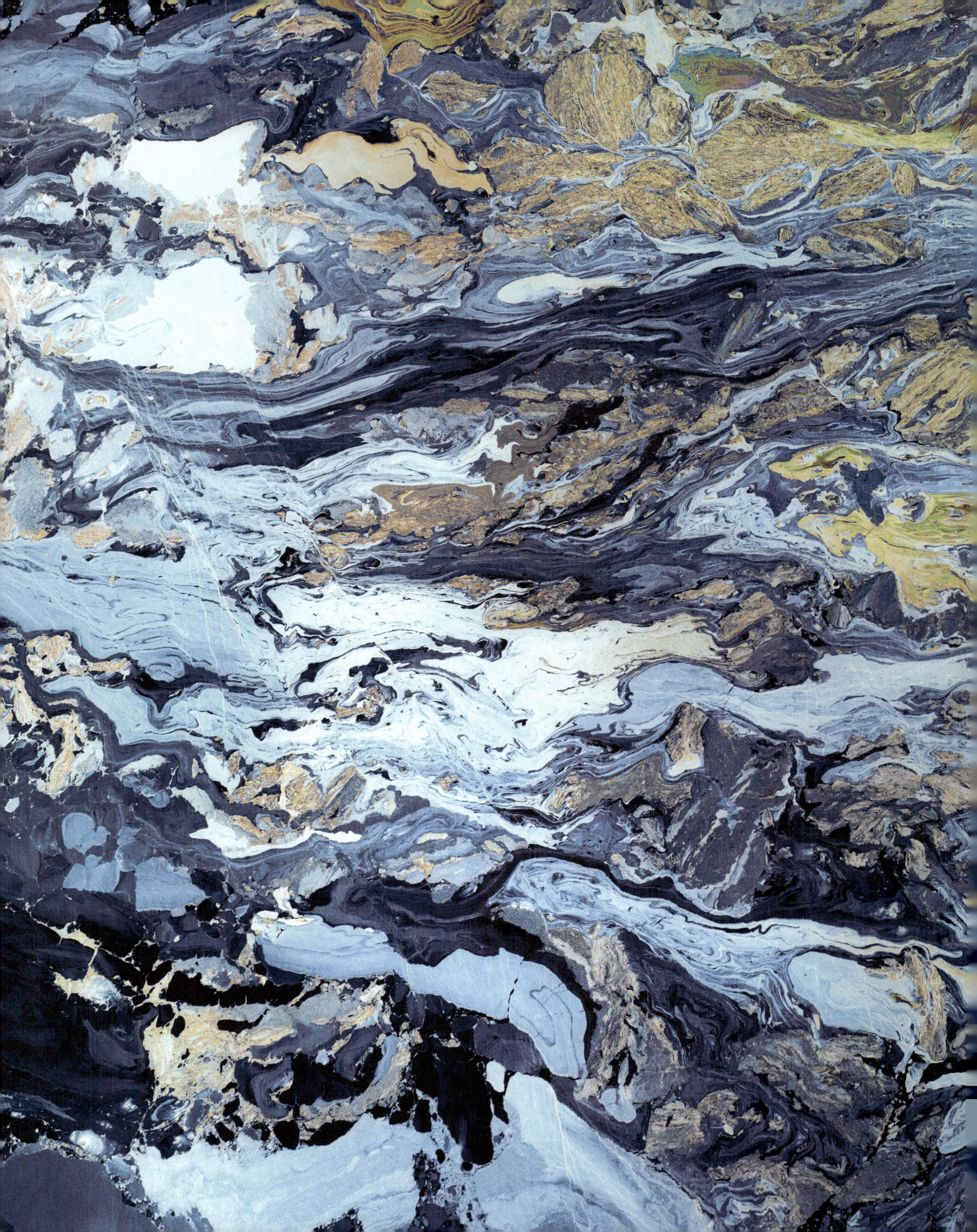